What Primary Teachers Should Know About

Music

FOR THE NATIONAL CURRICULUM

*This book is accompanied by a cassette which is available
from the publisher and book shops. The ISBN of the
cassette is 0 340 630892*

d'Reen Struthers

Hodder & Stoughton

A MEMBER OF THE HODDER HEADLINE GROUP

British Library Cataloguing in Publication Data

Struthers, d'Reen
What Primary Teachers Should Know About Music
for the National Curriculum. –
(Primary Bookshelf Series)
I. Title   II. Series
372.87

ISBN 0 340 621 249

First published 1994
Impression number   10 9 8 7 6 5 4 3 2 1
Year   1998 1997 1996 1995 1994

Typeset by Wearset, Boldon, Tyne and Wear.
Printed in Great Britain for Hodder & Stoughton Educational, a division of Hodder Headline Plc, 338 Euston Road, London NW1 3BH by The Bath Press, Lower Bristol Road, Bath.

Contents

To all children, some of whom I know have begun their musical journey in the womb and to Annie, who still continues to journey – musically and spiritually. Also, not least to my mother, who initiated my musical journey and has continued to believe in me.

Foreword

d'Reen Struthers has produced a comprehensive book that teachers will find extremely helpful. Starting from a historical context, she gives background information on the evolution of music in the school curriculum. In the chapters that follow, there are many practical suggestions on the teaching of music, and these are backed up by a well-produced audio tape.

A distinctive feature of this book is that throughout the sequence of suggested activities, we are always asked to think about the nature of the activity and to put ourselves in the place of the learner.

This book is more than a random collection of material and suggestions for the classroom. It is a systematically worked-out approach to music education in the primary school and, as such, will give many teachers valuable insights into the integrity of musical experience and its essential manageability in schools.

Keith Swanwick
Professor of Music Education
Institute of Education, University of London

Acknowledgements

Many people have helped to develop my thinking about music education; not least the many children in New Zealand, Scotland and England who have inspired my quest to seek ways of making musical experiences accessible to them.

Thanks should also be given to the numerous colleagues who, over the years, have debated issues and encouraged me to clarify and articulate my thoughts. In particular I would like to thank Professor Keith Swanwick, who not only wrote the Foreword to this book but who supervised my MA in Music Education (1981/82); Hilary Knight for being the first reader of my drafts; Rosemary Mitchell for acting as an informed sounding-board; Colum O'Clerigh, Jill Scarfe and Jane Southcott, for believing in me over the years; and Orde Eliason for taking the photographs for this book. The photographs were taken in Colville Primary School, London, with grateful thanks.

Friends, too many to name, also deserve acknowledgement. They have contributed their support over the years to various musical adventures, culminating in this project.

Finally, I acknowledge the support, sacrifice and understanding given by my partner while this book was being written. Thank you for walking the dog, helping with the housework, preparing all those meals, for being there when I needed you and for disappearing when I needed space.

For the right to reproduce copyright material thank you to:
HMSO and the controller of Her Majesty's Stationery Office for extracts from the 'Report of the Committee on the Supply, Recruitment and Training of Music Teachers'; 'Music for All Ages 5 to 14, Final Report of the Working Party on Music'; and 'Music in the National Curriculum'. To Professor Keith Swanwick for extracts taken from the United Kingdom Council for Music Education and Training (UKMET) Newsletter, February 1992, and from NFER, 1979; Teachers College Press, Columbia University for an extract reprinted by permission of the publisher from Tait, M. and Haack, P., *Principles and Processes of Music Education*, p.22, (1984, out of print); the Music Educators Journal (MENC) for an extract by Charles Leonhard; Inter Action for the right to reproduce d'Reen Struthers songs 'In the Darkness' and 'I can Stretch up very tall'; Cassell PLC, and editors Joanna Glover and Stephen Ward for an extract from *Teaching Music in the Primary School*; Rontledge (Publishers) and G. Brown and E.C. Wragg for an extract from p.10 of *Questioning*, in the 'Classroom Skills' Series; Brian Brocklehurst and Routledge (Publishers), for the extract from *Music in Schools*; the Calouste Gulbenkian Foundation for an extract from *The Arts in Schools, Principle, Practice and Provision*; the School Curriculum and Assessment Authority (SCAA) for the right to reproduce material from the National Curriculum Council's *Non-Statutory Guidance for Music*; Music Sales Ltd for the charts on pp.105–6, reproduced from *Starting Playing Creative Keyboard* (Wise Publications); and Cambridge University Press for an extract from p.32 of *Music in the Primary School*, by J. Mills.

For the audio tape accompanying this book, grateful thanks are extended to harmonia mundi uk Ltd for the right to use a 20 second excerpt from the Harmonia Mundi CD: *Gregorian Chant,*

The Deller Consort, (Catalogue number HMA190235/37); AKLOWA for the extract of recorded music from the tape by Felix Cobbson © 1982, Aklowa, African Heritage Village, Bishop's Stortford, Herts (full tape and New African Druming Pack available direct from AKLOWA); Anne Wild for a 20 second excerpt from the song 'A little ball of yarn' from the record Three Valley Folk (1971); Hangin's Too Good for Them (Julie McNamara, Elinor Harris and Trish Sweeney), for a 20 second excerpt of their performance of 'Farewell to Ireland'; and finally Louise Spooner for her skills as arranger, composer and technician and without whom the audio tape project would not have been considered feasible by the writer.

Introduction

Since the implementation of the National Curriculum in the UK in 1989, there have been many demands for change, both from within and outside the teaching profession. By 1993 the Government had accepted that an investigation was necessary and Sir Ron Dearing was appointed to consider the future of the National Curriculum and the existing assessment procedures.

The findings of Sir Ron Dearing included the suggestion that all curriculum subjects should be scaled down, with particular focus on Key Stage 2, where the National Curriculum was seen to be most heavily overloaded. Working parties were set up for this purpose and their Draft Proposals were launched to the public in early May 1994. Noticeably, there was a scaling down of the content as well as a clarification of the essential skills, knowledge and understanding which should be taught.

However, as the title of this book suggests I have addressed music for a National Curriculum context irrespective of any minor subsequent change. No matter what further alterations are made to the National Curriculum, the contexts, processes and procedures I deal with are still essential to any provision of musical experience and understanding.

In chapter 1, the reader is introduced to the historical context of music education in its various forms, as a part of an ever changing National Curriculum. The inclusion of music as part of the National Curriculum involves teachers in a challenge, which this publication aims to make less daunting.

Any book about music must seem incomplete without sound. **Chapter 2, entitled *Investigating Music*, is intended to be read in conjunction with the audio cassette accompanying this book**. Travelling along a directed musical journey, the reader will find many activities which could be adapted for use in classrooms, while at the same time gaining insights into what music is all about.

Chapter 3 focuses on the learner, discussing ways of involving the young learner in his or her own musical journey within the school context.

Whilst Chapter 4 *The teacher and pedagogy* reminds the reader that there will be many teaching strategies already used in other curriculum subjects which can also form an important part of teaching music. These will be expanded upon, with regards to how teachers can plan a music education programme and the various roles which they can adopt.

Teaching music is considered within the context of *The School* in Chapter 5. Here the role of a whole school approach to musical experience is considered.

Chapter 6 is entitled *Monitoring Music Progress*. Even before the introduction of the National Curriculum framework, teachers have always been involved in monitoring the work of their pupils. This process, is however, now recognised as being a crucial part of new moves to measure achievement, judge standards and ensure progression and development and must occur in every National Curriculum subject area.

The final chapter addresses the issue of *Resources*. At a time when school governors and teachers are being told to prioritise and account for their spending choices, we must ensure that music resources remain both appropriate and adequate.

Any National Curriculum document tabled about music, will imply certain views such as what is the 'role of music' in our society and 'what music should be valued?'. This publication however, attempts to move beyond political bias to address the question of what is involved in participating in musical experiences – either as a listener, performer or composer. It intends to offer the reader the opportunity to travel on a musical journey which could lay the foundation for a more general musical understanding. Happy travelling!

d'Reen Struthers

Approaching music in the National Curriculum

'Music education has a special and vital part to play in our society, and the rich amateur musical life our country enjoys is founded upon early encouragement and opportunity for young people.'
(David Mellor, as Secretary of State for National Heritage, 1992)

HISTORICAL OVERVIEW

Music has always been in our midst. We can trace evidence of this back to Ancient Greek and Roman times. In Britain, the earliest references to musical instruction have come from monastic records, some dating back to AD 600. However, we begin our general review from the eighteenth century. It is generally accepted from the writings at this time that only some sectors of the population had access to formal musical instruction. Apart from those who attended choir schools (which were set up to ensure that there were enough choristers for cathedral services (Bridge, 1918)), accounts of music being part of a school curriculum are restricted to a very few elite public schools (Hill, 1834). Indeed, music had generally been considered to be something of a pleasant pastime, not worthy of serious study, until the late eighteenth century, although it continued to be an important aspect of worship.

From a plea made by Bishop Porteous in 1790 to reform parochial psalmody, it is clear that even the state of music in churches was at a low ebb. He considered that children should be provided with rudimentary training in singing at schools, a reminder of early monastic schools which endorsed musical learning as a tool for improving the worship of the Lord and inculcating moral values (Winn, 1954). Because of the needs of the churches, singing was considered a 'useful' exercise.

At the turn of the nineteenth century, there were efforts to educate the 'lower orders' of the population. Charity schools and Sunday schools offered instruction in the three Rs. The Church began to dominate in the area of mass elementary education, and music was encouraged mainly to improve hymn singing.

'When it is considered that there are now three hundred thousand Sunday school children in various parts of the kingdom, if one-third of them can be taught to perform the psalm tunes tolerably well, these useful institutions will contribute no less to the improvement of parochial psalmody that to the reformation of the lower orders of the people.'
  (Porteous, 1811)

Manuals for instruction began to appear, such as that by John Turner, entitled *Manual of Instruction in Vocal Music: Chiefly with a view to Psalmody* (1833).

By the mid-nineteenth century, music was seen to serve other purposes besides those of worship alone. The great educational reformers, such as Rousseau, Pestalozzi and Froebel, all gave it an honoured place in their systems. It was Rousseau who re-discovered the Greek conception of music as a means of self-expression. In *Emile* he expressed certain views which were to influence the work of educational thinkers in Britain through to the present day. In writing about the education of Emile, Rousseau wrote:

'Man has three kinds of voice: namely the speaking or articulating voice, a singing or melodious voice, and the impassioned or modulated voice . . . In singing, we do hardly more than render the ideas of the others. Now in order to render them, we must be able to read them . . . Moreover, in order to know music well, it does not suffice to render it; it is necessary to compose it, and one should be learned along with the other, for except in this way music is never learned very well.'
  (Rousseau, 1906)

Robert Owen, founder of the model New Lanark School (1816) was most impressed when he visited schools on the continent and saw for himself the educational philosophies of both Rousseau and Pestalozzi. Both realised that children needed to be treated as children and not as adults in miniature. Owen's schools, therefore,

included music and dancing on the curriculum in a manner that took account of the child's world – clapping to the beat while singing a nursery rhyme rather than being drilled and puzzled by the learning of crotchets and quavers. Owen's schools became model schools for the rest of England.

From the beginning of the nineteenth century, sight-singing was becoming a key part of the school and community. Teaching methods were being adopted from the continent with state backing. New manuals were being printed, and by 1841 a 'method of teaching singing' had been officially adopted by the Board of Education. The 'official' method was to change again some ten years later to a system known as the Curwen method, adopted from the successful work of Sara Glover. So it was that 'tonic sol-fa' became established in schools under the Elementary Education Act of 1840.

The country's fervour for sight-singing is accounted for in numerous reports of annual gatherings in St Paul's Cathedral and at Crystal Palace. Massed choir events were held up until 1877. These consisted of choirs, four thousand strong, from the London 'charity' schools, singing metrical psalms and items from the works of Handel and Coronation Hymns, all written in sol-fa form.

Shortly after the passing of the Forester Act of 1870, singing virtually became a compulsory subject of elementary education in all Board Schools (one-sixth of the annual grant being payable only if singing was included in the school curriculum). The code of 1882 introduced what is commonly referred to as a 'payment by results' scheme – sixpence for every pupil who had rote learnt a specific number of songs and a shilling for singing by sight from notation.

Between 1870 and 1900, the class teacher, trained in a teachers' college to use Curwen's tonic sol-fa method, taught music in elementary schools. But by the end of the century, the craft of teaching sight-singing had begun to decline as both teaching methods and curriculum content began to expand. There was also a need for more suitable songs, especially for younger children. Collections of songs from earlier centuries were collated. Shortly after the turn of the century, the Board of Education gave official backing to a song repertory based on these traditional sources. Its *Suggestions for the Consideration of Teachers*, first published in 1905, included an appendix containing a lengthy list of recommended English, Scottish, Welsh and Irish songs, with a few rounds. Songs collected from oral traditions then added a wealth of folk music to the repertoire in later years. The introduction of the School Music Festival – the Association of Competitive Festivals was founded in 1905; the British Federation of Music Festivals in 1921; and the Non-competitive Festival Movements began in 1927 – increased the search for satisfactory repertoire, while bringing top composers and conductors into closer contact with elementary schools. This not only led to improved standards of singing but also the composition of music for children's voices.

A visiting composer, Zoltan Kodaly, was impressed by the quality of singing he found in English schools. On his return to Hungary, he adapted the Curwen method and collected and composed music based on the Hungarian folk tradition. His approach was later to find its way back to England in the late 1960s when school singing was in decline.

The Victorian era also saw the rise of private music lessons, which occurred in the drawing rooms of the monied classes (Taylor, 1979) from the late nineteenth century onwards. Mass-produced pianos and violins generated a demand for tuition. Teachers would advertise themselves for private tuition both in homes and larger public schools, where musical traditions would include instrumental lessons from visiting teachers. This extra-curricular aspect of music tuition appears to have been reinforced by students being offered the opportunity to take local music examinations as external students with Trinity College (1876), and later the Royal

Academy and the Royal College.

By 1925, Arnold Dolmetsch had successfully mass-produced the descant recorder, and it was being purchased by schools. The 'Pipers Guild' at this time was also encouraging children to both make and play bamboo pipes.

Up until the time of the gramophone being invented in the late nineteenth century, access to musical performances was restricted to those who could afford to pay to see visiting musicians. Select private schools, who had the financial resources to employ highly qualified musicians/ teachers, were able to offer their pupils not only individual tuition, but also school orchestras, chamber music groups and chapel services.

After the First World War, there was a gradual decline in the teaching of singing and musical theory. Instead, more emphasis was placed on the need for the enjoyment and appreciation of music. Concern was mounting for the establishment of 'intelligent listening habits for life'. Concerts specifically designed for children were organised, and publications of aural training began to appear. By 1927, the title of the Board of Education's Handbook, *Suggestions for the Consideration of Teachers: The teaching of singing*, had been changed so that singing was no longer given such a focus. Instead, the word 'music' appeared after the colon.

By 1933, the Board of Education's *Recent Developments in School Music* was suggesting that a school of any size was not properly equipped if it did not possess a gramophone and a good stock of records. However, concerns were being raised in the same year about the disadvantages of the 'listening' aspect of music. An official report from Cambridgeshire recommended that the balance of the music curriculum needed to be redressed on the side of practical work as against the less constructive art of passive listening.

Radio broadcasts devised specially for schools began in 1924. These acted as a substitute where no specialised music teaching was available, assisting the general class teacher with ideas and repertoire.

By the mid-1930s, the well-known *Music and Movement* radio lessons had begun, and were a feature of most elementary schools. For some, this programme enabled teachers to feel they had covered two necessary elements of the recommended syllabus of the day. Indeed, it is also significant that in secondary schools, the introduction of external examinations in 1917 had left music as a subject relegated to 'group four' with no 'matriculation' status for university entrance. The group system enabled some subjects to be given higher status than others for the purpose of university selection. Other 'group four' subjects included domestic science, art and handicraft. Since this time, the concept of 'music as an optional extra' has been hard to extinguish. Similarly, the status accorded to music in the secondary school had an impact on what provision was seen as necessary, or even desirable, in the elementary school.

External influences continued to affect music in schools – not least the rise, after the wars, of a growing mass-education movement which included music societies, associations and clubs. Children were being given every opportunity to sing and participate in choral festivals, but many had limited access to instrumental tuition. There is evidence to suggest that the playing of instruments formed no appreciable part of music-making in the elementary school, although 'percussion instruments had been used to accompany a form of music drill' (Taylor, 1979) in some schools. The recorder, with its greater melodic range, rapidly became the alternative to the percussion band, being both affordable and readily available.

In the two decades following the Second World War, many changes in all aspects of education can be noted. The McNair Report of 1944 stated:

'. . . the present state of music in the grammar school . . . is the most potent cause of the short supply of music teachers for the schools . . . The poor standard of music in so many secondary (grammar) schools and the lack of adequate opportunities for the musical education of those with exceptional gifts means that hundreds of potential teachers of music are lost.'
(HMSO, 1944)

Continuity and structure were being called for by 1954. Dr J. Mainwaring, in his book *Teaching Music in Schools* (Mainwaring, 1954), stressed that a child's musical experience in school should be of a continuous, progressive and purposeful kind, and should form part of a coherent and consistently pursued plan of musical development.

Brocklehurst, writing in 1962, suggested that the situation was no better. He looked at junior schools and found there was still a shortage of musically accomplished teachers. He also observed that head teachers of junior schools were often handicapped by poor resources and great pressures from parents, obsessed with the idea of their children securing grammar school places. Music was seen as the 'frill' which could be readily dismissed in favour of those subjects given more 'weighting' by the grammar schools (Brocklehurst, 1962).

The late 1950s saw the introduction of instruments developed by the German educator Carl Orff. Orff introduced the idea that young children should be engaged not only with simple untuned instruments, but also with tuned instruments from an early age. His work led him to develop the collection of easy-to-use tuned percussion instruments now commonly found in schools – xylophones, glockenspiels and metallophones – as well as encouraging the mass production of easy-to-handle smaller percussion instruments into British schools.

This coincided with the expansion of teacher training establishments and music departments within them. School television programmes began in 1957, with the first music programme commencing in 1963. This coincided with the increased focus being given to practical music-making, now possible with the imported Orff instruments. Indeed, during the next decade music teachers began to offer pupils more opportunities to 'create' their own musical forms. This often meant a departure from class singing to classes including music-making; a switch from passive listening to active participation in composing and performing.

With the gradual expansion of local instrumental services funded by Local Education Authorities (LEAs), there were increased opportunities for children of all backgrounds to learn an instrument. Saturday music schools, local orchestras, bands and choirs expanded and absorbed the growing number of young musical enthusiasts.

For many, however, the quality of the music lesson was very much at the mercy of the skills, confidence and enthusiasms of the staff and the organisational support and prioritisation of music made by the head teacher. While singing remained for some the major source of musical activity, other schools welcomed the LEA's peripatetic instrumental music staff, who usually provided instruments on loan and free lessons. Some schools were staffed with a music specialist who only took music throughout the school. In these instances, there were usually numerous extra-curricular musical activities offered.

Theories that children should not be pestered to learn to spell, write grammatically or learn multiplication tables later found a musical counterpart in arguments against teaching the use of notation, the creative music-making argument. It was felt that more enjoyable musical activities should be pursued. By the mid-1980s, falling rolls and the move towards increased accountability led to many such music specialists being required to take on ordinary classroom duties. With this, the range of musical opportunities available was reduced. By now, teachers who were at school during this rise of creative music-making were now being trained. Many were more confident than their predecessors and were inclined to 'try and compose a piece' with instruments rather than to

sing and vocally improvise. Initial teacher education establishments were able to provide only limited music courses for generalist teachers, some even being optional. Similarly, the expanding school curriculum with many new subject areas meant that the allocation of music on the school timetable remained similar to that which had existed a century earlier.

The range of musical activities possible and acceptable had also expanded. Instead of producing a general broadening of the music curriculum, the range of alternative procedures presented to teachers meant that decisions had to be made about what to include and what to omit in the time available.

The 1980s saw an increasing drive towards a complete curriculum reshuffle. For music, this included a change to the GCSE examination. Now such elements as composition and continuous assessment and a broadening of repertoire/styles were included. More students began to opt for music. These changes to secondary school music encouraged more young people to opt for the subject. However, coping with pupils from numerous feeder schools, often meant that the secondary music specialist preferred to assume all pupils had a limited range of musical experiences in their primary schools. For many, however, what was now acceptable in the secondary school examination, could be seen as acceptable in the junior school. LEA instrumental services were threatened and the teaching profession generally felt criticised and under threat.

MUSICAL EXPERIENCES IN PRIMARY SCHOOLS

There are many books which discuss musical experiences in the primary school. Most describe these experiences in terms of activities for the learners, usually with the understanding that the activities will be offered 'for all'. Indeed, the term 'music for all' has had a familiar ring to it for many years.

With the introduction of the Education Reform Act (ERA) of 1988, significant changes have been necessary to all aspects of teaching. While the profession has always catered for individual needs, terms such as 'differentiation' require explicit planning for each pupil's requirements. The process of assessment, which the ERA also highlights, requires that teachers take account of each pupil's level of attainment.

In music, we must, therefore, think not of 'music for all' but 'music for each'. This change should have a significant impact on how we teach music. We need to be much more aware about who the learners are and what musical processes they are actively engaged in. A mass singing event will no longer be enough. Indeed, this change reaffirms the core of our professional task in the classroom. As with other subject areas, we need to focus more on how pupils are learning, and select teaching strategies that will facilitate individual growth and development.

THE INTRODUCTION OF THE NATIONAL CURRICULUM

In the past, we have seen how a supportive head teacher or a teaching post given over to a music specialist has meant that music in school has thrived. Unlike former times, when it has sometimes been necessary to argue the rightful place of music on the timetable, the National Curriculum in Britain (introduced with the Education Reform Act of 1988) now includes music as one of the six foundation subjects.

The Education Reform Act 1988 empowers the Secretaries of State to specify Attainment Targets, End of Key Stage Statements (EOKSS) and Programmes of Study. Before they may draft Orders, they are required to make formal proposals in accordance with the provisions of the Act. In England, the Secretary of State for Education and Science is required to make proposals to the National Curriculum Council (NCC), which in turn is required to consult and then to make a report to the Secretary of State, containing a summary of views expressed on his proposals and the NCC's advice and recommendations.

It could be argued that one of the benefits of a National Curriculum is a formalised statutory content. For the first time since 1841, when the Wilhelm method of teaching singing was given official blessing by the Board of Education, a consensus among music educators in Britain about the processes and content for a music curriculum has been reached.

> 'I am gratified to note the high degree of participation and consensus among every branch of the Council and it is hoped that the strength of professional opinion which the Council's response represents will be respected in what may, unfortunately, become a highly politicised context.'
> (Prof. K. Swanwick, as Chair of UKCMET, February 1992)

A final Report was submitted to the Secretary of State for Education in June 1991 and made available for general comment. After a consultation period of three months, as laid down by the Act, the Secretary of State's comments on the Report of the Music Working group (which they set up to make recommendations on Attainment Targets and Programmes of Study) were published as 'Music for ages 5 to 14' in August 1991.

After a consultation period, there was a noticeable reduction from four to three Attainment Targets. 'Performing, composing, listening and knowing' became 'performing, composing and appraising'. This change was supported by 80 per cent of those who responded to the Secretary of State, while only 6 per cent supported a reduction to two Attainment Targets. The National Curriculum Council was to ignore the popular view, and printed its own document with only two Attainment Targets, AT1: 'Performing and composing'; and AT2: 'Knowledge and understanding'. A massive lobby and mobilisation of support from among musicians, conductors, academics and teachers led to the NCC document being slightly altered. The present music orders appeared in January 1992. There are two Attainment Targets, AT1: 'Performing and composing'; and AT2: 'Listening and appraising'.

Another area of concern must be mentioned. In 1985, the benefit to learning of a culturally diverse music curriculum was identified by Her Majesty's Inspectors with the publication of an important document to music teachers, *Curriculum Matters 4 – Music from 5 to 16* (HMI, 1985), which clearly acknowledges that pupils' understanding is enhanced through experiencing a wide-ranging repertoire. It recommended that all children should be directed towards developing:

> 'a greater awareness of musical similarities and differences between cultures and of the enrichment which can come from sharing them.'
> (para. 19)

Six years later, the Interim Report fully endorsed the findings of previous research and supported the need for children to experience a multitude of musical genres. Despite the high level of support given by educationalists and the music profession, it was rejected and re-written into Parliamentary Orders with very different objectives. The Parliamentary Orders for music have removed the inclusive language of the Working Group's Interim and Final Reports, which embraced all music. We are now left with a predominance of Western music examples in the orders, expressed in a language which suggests that 'other' musics are readily generalisable and 'foreign'. The paragraphs which have been removed or drastically amended are the ones consistently reinforcing the importance of pupils being given the opportunities, encouraged, able to justify preferences and able to express their own reasoned opinions. With the Parliamentary Orders strongly urging the study of the Western classical tradition, there is an underlying message about which music is to be valued, as well as a clear viewpoint about what is British and should, therefore, be passed on to future generations.

> 'Such an attitude not only demotivates black children (children from other cultural backgrounds) but also robs white children (actually restricts the opportunities for all children) of the opportunity of finding music from all over the world that thrills them.'
> (Moulton, 1992)

The Draft Proposals (1994) have retained the clumsy language around repertoire. However with the Key Stage-specific programmes of study now having more clarity, it may even be the case that the sentence below for Key Stage 2 is altered after further consultation:

> 'It should include music in a variety of styles, taken from: the European "classical" tradition; folk and popular music; the countries and regions of the British Isles; a variety of cultures; and should include music by well-known composers and performers.'

THE CHALLENGE

'Music education should be mainly concerned with bringing children into contact with the musician's fundamental activities of performing, composing and listening.' (HMI, 1985a, p. 2)

Certainly, there is a challenge! In ways never before seen on the statute books, teachers in primary schools are required to provide music as a foundation subject. The content of the music curriculum has been stipulated in the form of a General Programme of Study which begins 'Pupils should be given opportunities to' and a Key Stage-specific Programme of Study which states 'Pupils should be taught to'. Therefore, the challenge facing all primary teachers is to be a mediator between the pupils and the content of the National Curriculum. How can we respond to this challenge?

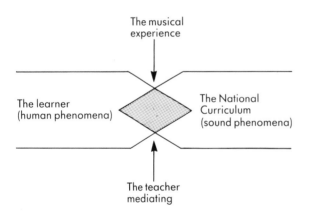

Figure 1   Components of teaching music

Functioning in this role as mediator, the teacher needs to consider ways in which he or she can enhance the musical experiences of the learners. This book is based on the belief that music and people can interact in very special ways, but for this to happen, people must meet music purposefully in an educational atmosphere. While casual interaction may yield some positive and pleasing effects, carefully planned interaction

through education can bring about profoundly beneficial and deeply satisfying results. It is this carefully planned interaction that should characterise music education. The interaction becomes the experience, and the experience is at the heart of the educational process.

This challenge appears for all other areas of experience too – the government prefers to refer to 'subject areas'. Teachers are required to bring their professional understanding of the learning and teaching process forward into this mediator role. To have an expert knowledge of all the subjects found on the National Curriculum is impractical.

However, by building on their professional knowledge as educators, teachers are able to apply their understanding of the ways children learn to their personal framework of understanding about the curriculum 'subject' areas. This book is, therefore, about a journey. Travelling through each chapter, the reader will be able to develop their professional knowledge as it applies to teaching music. I have attempted to provide a framework or scaffolding which teachers can use to assist them in approaching the teaching of music for the National Curriculum.

The components of figure 1 are therefore vital. As our aim is to enhance the quality of the musical experiences we provide for our pupils, we need to:

- Qualify our understanding of children's learning and discover how it applies to their learning music.
- Have a way of approaching the nature of music, and discover what processes are involved – maybe other subjects may share the use of similar ones?
- Make use of our professional understanding about how to manage the learning situation, how to cater for individual needs and how to respond to the musical utterances pupils make, keeping records which will show pupil achievement and advancement.

Chapter 2 will begin the journey by investigating 'music', in close association with the accompanying audio tape.

SUGGESTIONS

1 Can you recall your own encounters with music at school? In what way did they conform to the historical overview given in pages 13–20?

2 Make a list of what you can remember 'doing' during music at school. How much of your list involved composing, performing and/or appraising?

3 In what ways do you feel music today has changed? Should any changes you have identified be incorporated into the music programme in your school?

4 'In a quite frightening way, teachers stand between pupils and music, sometimes acting as a window or an open door but at other times functioning only as an impediment, blocking off access to music itself.'
(Swanwick, K. and Taylor, D., 1982, p. 7)

Prepare a list of things which you think teachers do unintentionally, which put pupils off finding music exciting.

Investigating music

'Music may be experienced as a continuum from objective acoustical phenomena to subjective psychological experiences. It can be thought-provoking, feeling-provoking, or a combination of both. Because music is a sociocultural phenomenon, it is also a sharing experience, even when one is performing it or hearing it alone.'
(Tait and Haack, 1984, p. 22)

When I asked 'What is music?' at an Inset day recently, a teacher said 'organisation out of the chaos of sound'. This definition received lots of cheers. Further statements, including words such as pattern, rhythm, pitch and voices, were also received. Note the first statement implies that the organisation or form chosen in some way relieves us from the feeling of chaos. In addition, this would suggest that 'how' the sounds have been heard by the listener, the meaning that has been comprehended, the sense that has been made, is also an important aspect of clarifying what is music. It is true that I might appreciate listening to Wagner at certain times, but that on a Sunday morning after a good dinner party the night before, I might not appreciate being able to hear the neighbours version of it. In this instance, I would not be appreciating the 'whole' form, let alone enjoying the steady slow underlying pulse.

So in beginning to consider 'What is music?', we must try to ensure that our approach does not detract from the wonderment and power of music. Some would say that the elements and forms of music have often been presented or studied in an overly analytical and simplistic fashion, without taking into account many of the relationships that are generated between the elements and within the forms, relationships that are largely responsible for any resulting aesthetic properties. The process is similar to a lesson in human biology; simply labelling the parts of the body will not necessarily increase one's insight into the miracle of life. Just as humans are more than just a collection of bones, muscles and nerves, so music is more than a collection of rhythms, melodies and harmonies. It is for this reason that emphasis is placed on the aesthetic properties of music. Such properties can be defined as the comprehensive shapes and patterns of music that emerge from the relationships of the elements and forms. A well-known ethnomusicologist, John Blacking, wrote:

'Music is humanly organised sound . . . intended for other human ears . . . concerned with communication and relationships between people.'
(Blacking, 1976, pp. 11–12)

The National Curriculum requires us to have a good understanding about what these fundamental elements are, before we can begin to hear how they are used in combination to create numerous 'forms' and, indeed, go on and be able to talk about them in an 'appraising' manner.

THE ELEMENTS OF MUSIC

The musical elements appear in the Introductory Statement for each Key Stage, emphasising their central role in all musical activities.

'Elements: One of the fundamental components of a larger musical unit. Elements which are primarily *expressive*, such as melody, harmony, rhythm, pace, timbre, texture, dynamics, articulation and silence, manifest emotions, feelings and ideas. The ways in which they are ordered may also contribute to the structure of music. Elements which are primarily *structural*, such as pitch, interval, motif, phrase, chord, cadence, pulse, duration, structure and form, are arranged and interrelated to create a musical construction. They may also contribute to the

expression of emotions, feelings and ideas.' (DES, 1991)

For the purposes of the 'conceptual framework' which this book proposes (see Chapter 4), the order of the elements has been slightly altered.

This section will provide aural examples with further written explanations to help describe what the terms mean. (I suggest that you read the text and then listen to the accompanying track on the tape. The figures will help your 'hearing' and you are invited to respond to the questions which are asked.)

Chapters 3 and 4 will return to the examples cited here, with additional suggestions for classroom activities and extensions.

ELEMENTS	KEY STAGE 1	KEY STAGE 2
duration	pulse; rhythm; long—short sounds	pulse; metre and rhythm
structure	pattern; repetition/contrast	different ways sounds are organised in simple forms; phrase; repetition; contrast; ostinato (a musical pattern which is repeated many times); melody
dynamics	loud—quiet silence	different levels of volume; accents; silence
speed/tempo	fast—slow	gradations of speed
timbre	quality of sound	different qualities of sound
pitch	high—low	melody; chords
texture	one sound or several sounds	different ways sounds are put together; melody and accompaniment

Figure 2   The elements of music as taken from the Introductory Statements, Draft Proposals (1994)

TAPE: TRACKS 1–9 (DURATION)

Track 1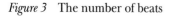

This musical element refers to the overall organisation of sound into time groups. You will no doubt know that a waltz and a march are different forms and, of course, we can move in different ways to them. There are many different 'forms' of organising sound in time. Most cultures have their own unique forms for different occasions or for different moods.

Just as our hearts beat in a regular manner, so too can sounds be organised to match the steady pulse pattern. On this first track you will hear a steady beat (like a pulse) played on a bass drum. To this is added some music from a range of cultures. As you listen, tap along with the bass drum and feel the pulse within the music. In order you will hear:

1	Irish	5	Indian
2	Latin American	6	pop music
3	Greek	7	baroque music
4	English folk		

Track 2 ▣

Sometimes this beat is marked out into groups of two, three or four. Listen to the four examples on the tape. See if you can 'feel' how many beats there are. In other words, would you be counting one...two...three, one...two...three or one...two...three...four..., one...two...three...four? Answers p. 49.

TRACK	Nº OF BEATS
2 a	
b	
c	
d	

Figure 3   The number of beats

Track 3 ▣

On track three you will hear three other examples where there is no discernible pulse. First, part of a Gregorian chant. Secondly, a group of children playing instruments and, finally, some 'wind' music.

Track 4 ▣

Listen now for the children's performance from the previous track being played with a pulse. You will hear how the maintenance of a steady beat by all players adds to the cohesion of the sounds and actually gives the same piece not only organisation, but also a significant identity of its own – a meaning.

Track 5 ▣

When we speak of metre in poetry, we are referring to where there is a feeling of weighting. It is this weighting (some might say 'accent') that highlights certain words, giving a particular meaning to the phrases. Consider the following, which you will also hear spoken on the tape:

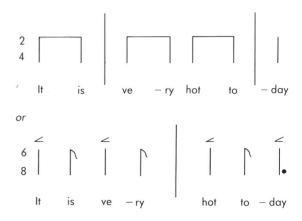

Figure 4   Weighting or accent of words

Track 6

Developing this idea, consider 'Polly put the kettle on'. There are three versions on track six, shown in figures 5–7.

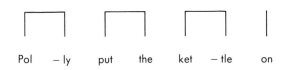

Pol – ly put the ket – tle on

Figure 5 Different rhythms, invoke different meanings and feelings–'Polly put the kettle on' (first time)

In the first example, there is an immediate sense of movement, heading towards 'on', which is where the movement is 'still' for a moment. One can almost perceive the little footsteps in a running pattern. The second example, feels very different. As we do not normally say the word 'kettle' in that manner, it surprises us and certainly alters the feeling of the statement or phrase.

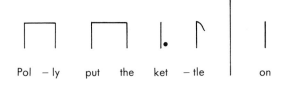

Pol – ly put the ket – tle on

Figure 6 'Polly put the kettle on' (second time)

In the third example, we find the pattern picks up the first syllable of those words in the phrase which are significant. There is a 'skipping', almost bouncing, feel to the pattern.

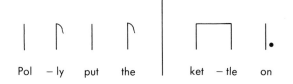

Pol – ly put the ket – tle on

Figure 7 'Polly put the kettle on' (third time)

We could ask if this is very appropriate for a 'full kettle of water'? This might lead us back to the first example, where the metre enabled us to feel a 'smoother', more continuous line in the melody (examples 1 & 3 are repeated on the tape).

What you have been hearing is how sounds can be given different durations. Some sounds are shorter or longer than others, and can be combined in numerous ways. Of course, where no words exist, it is not *linguistic* sense or meaning, but an *aural* sense that we are working with. If you like, we are dealing with perception; the messages and meanings we take from what we perceive. You will now hear 'Polly put the kettle on' organised in a way that uses a different metre or beat, via the convention of organising the notes in a different rhythmic sequence. This most definitely produces a different 'feel'. As you listen, hear how some notes have been lengthened and others shortened, and how this can alter the 'feel' of this traditional nursery rhyme.

Track 7

To revisit this notion of beat and rhythm, let us take an example from a classroom activity. As you read aloud the names below, clap a steady pulse:

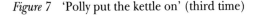
Mark   Jasvinder   Jasmine   and   Tony

Figure 8 Steady pulse

The pulse, or metre, we have set up is steady, occurring at regular intervals and is, indeed, 'pulse-like' with a feel of four about it. If we were to clap the syllables of the words, we would in effect, be clapping a rhythmic pattern.

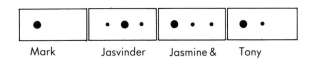

Mark   Jasvinder   Jasmine &   Tony

Figure 9 Rhythmic pattern around the pulse

Of course, we could make up sentences for all sorts of things depending on our theme or topic.

Your sentences may have a feel of any number, so long as it is steady.

On the other hand, without words we could also play sound patterns that represent different movements, for example, walking, running, skipping, hopping, creeping. Of course, words are very helpful; they can immediately convey meaning and often can be written in ways that help to convey the 'musical' sense, for example:

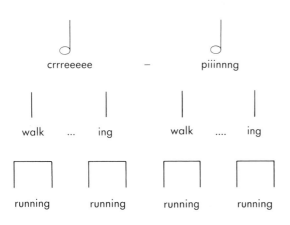

Figure 10   Sound patterns

This is where it is possible to see the relationship between mathematics and music.

This kind of understanding makes the comprehension of musical notation seem less daunting – each sound is usually taken as a measure of a whole, which is predetermined by

the 'time signature' which we find at the start of a piece of music:

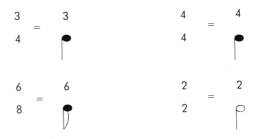

Figure 12   Time signature

Track 8

Long and short sounds cannot necessarily be made on every instrument. Consider the following instruments while you listen to Track 8:

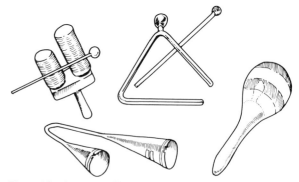

Figure 13   A range of instruments can produce short or long sounds

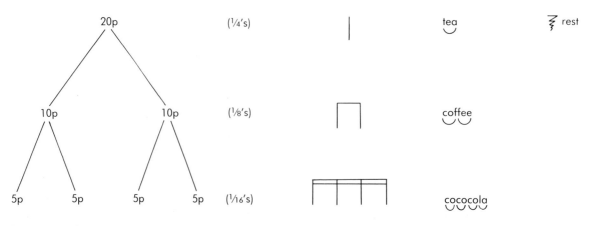

Figure 11   Relationship between mathematics and music

Not every instrument is capable of producing a long sound. This is why at pre-Key Stage 1 it is important to encourage the children to experiment with different instruments and group them in terms of:

- how they are played (tapped, shaken, blown, scraped, plucked)
- what they are made of (wood, metal, plastic, ceramic)
- whether they can make long or short sounds
- dull or bright sounds
- one or more sounds, etc.

Track 9 🔲

Listen to another collection of instruments on the tape. After the first hearing, pause the tape and identify whether each of the sounds was long or short.

TRACK	LONG	SHORT	INSTRUMENT
9 1			
2			
3			
4			

Figure 14 Record your results in the table

During the second hearing, note below which instrument corresponds to which sound. Answers on p. 49.

Figure 15 Which instrument corresponds with which sound on the tape?

With this information, we are now in a position to be able to select the most appropriate instruments for a composition with long or short sounds.

TAPE: TRACKS 10–19 (STRUCTURE)

Professor Keith Swanwick reminds us that, for sounds to become music, there are three necessary conditions which need to be fulfilled:

'1. Selection: Not every available sound is used; many are rejected and some are repeated a great deal.
2. Relation: The sounds are made to combine or to precede or follow each other in time.

3. Intention: The composer/performer intends to make music (whatever it is) and we intend to hear it.'
(Swanwick, 1979, p. 9)

We have already begun to consider the different sounds that can be selected in terms of their duration, and the way sounds of varying lengths can be placed alongside each other. We have also seen that moods and feelings can be conveyed intentionally by selecting a particular metre and rhythmic pattern.

Having now worked with both beat and rhythm, how can these two elements work together in music? First, we need to decide on what mood or 'feel' we want to generate. Let us use an example which might also be useful in a classroom. As most young children can walk, but not all can skip, we shall begin with the feel of a march. For this, the pulse will be even, and the rhythmic pattern should match the pulse, in even steady measures.

Track 10

Consider these two examples. While listening, try and imagine yourself marching along in a parade to them. Is one more 'march-like' than the other? Why could this be? Was it the selection of instruments used? Were they different? Was it the pulse? Which example felt less like a march – can you say why? Answers on p. 49.

Track 11

Building on this notion with more examples of nursery rhymes, notice how some are structured so we could walk to them, others we could jog to, while still others appear to have more of a skipping or galloping 'feel' about them. I have given a few under each heading. Try saying them through, feeling the pulse alongside the rhythmic pattern. Can you add others to these lists?

WALK

'Grand old Duke of York''

'Baa baa black sheep'

'Twinkle twinkle'

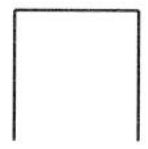

JOGGING

'Polly put the kettle on'

'In and out the dusty bluebells'

'I'm a little teapot'

GALL' a – PING a'

'Jack and Jill'

'Humpty Dumpty'

'Incy wincy spider'

Figure 16   Patterns of some nursery rhymes

Track 12

Another aspect to our making sense of the sounds as they are organised is in the use of phrases. A phrase is a part of a musical sentence, a subsection (as a phrase in language is part of a sentence). It is often thought of as the place where the instrumental player breathes. We shall consider some examples:

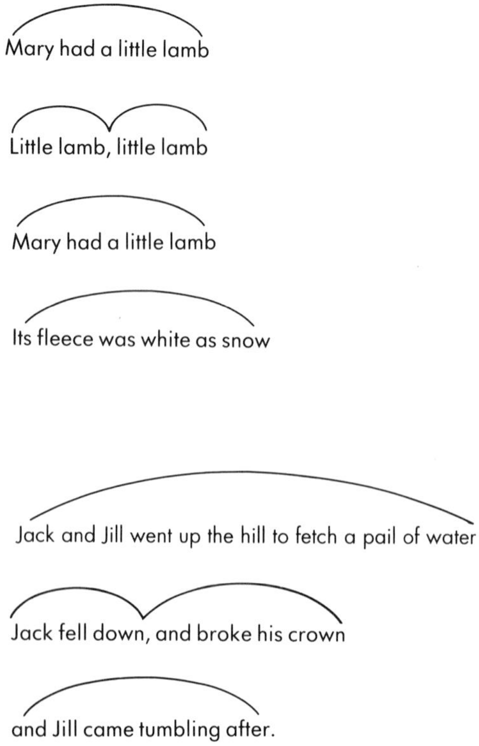

Mary had a little lamb

Little lamb, little lamb

Mary had a little lamb

Its fleece was white as snow

Jack and Jill went up the hill to fetch a pail of water

Jack fell down, and broke his crown

and Jill came tumbling after.

Figure 17   Phrases are parts of musical sentences

The musical structures of these two rhymes are different; two distinct forms and feelings can be perceived.

Track 13 ▣

Many songs are organised with a repeated chorus and a verse. This 'structure' is very common. The 'echo' structure, where a phrase is repeated, can be found in the nursery rhyme 'Frère Jacque' (sometimes known as 'Are you sleeping?').

Track 14 ▣

Then there is the 'question and answer' structure as demonstrated on this track.

Track 15 ▣

Repetition and contrast are other structural devices often used by composers. Listen out in this track for the pitch and rhythmic pattern that is repeated, then for the contrasting phrase and, finally, the return of the first pattern to conclude the piece. As it is played twice, try on the second hearing to tap the pulse in accompaniment.

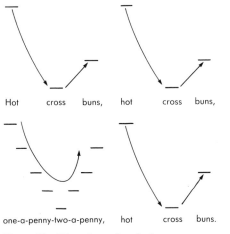

Figure 18 Direction of melody

Track 16 ▣

This next track uses several of the structural conventions we have considered. In particular, hear how a pattern is revisited numerous times, interspersed with variations or contrasts. This gives the identifiable form: A B A C A A. Of course, for convenience and length, we have used repeated and contrasted musical phrases. In much longer works, you can find whole sections being given the label A or B, as in a 'simple ternary form'. The track you will hear is written in the style of a 'gavotte' – otherwise known as an Elizabethan Dance.

Track 17 ▣

Sometimes there is no obvious return to the familiar pattern. One may begin with a motif, musical phrase or, sometimes, a musical sentence, which then begins to be 'worked' on in numerous ways. In this track, you will hear the 'theme and variations' of the nursery rhyme 'Baa baa black sheep'. After the main theme has been played, we begin to deviate away from it. You will be able to hear it played back to front, played in another key (*transposed*), played within different pulse groups, and even a Chinese version. You might like to try to spot the differences and similarities. Your pupils may also enjoy this activity.

Figure 19 Various ways of playing 'Baa baa black sheep'

Track 18 📼

As with a good story, musical compositions require thought about how they are going to begin, what will happen during them, and how they will end. We are working with the four rhythmic groupings introduced in the section entitled 'Duration' (see pp. 24–7):

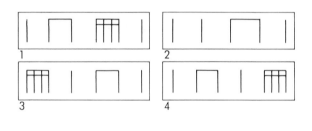

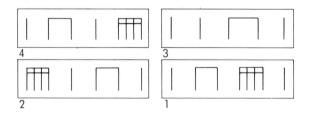

Figure 20 Rhythmic groupings

These four 'bars' need to be organised. How does it sound going from numbers 1–4? What happens if we changed the order of the bars (that is, bars 4–2–3–1)? Listen to the overall structure of the piece. Is there a feeling of completion

about the first trial (1–2–3–4) or the second? Is this feeling improved by jiggling the bars around? (4–2–3–1)? Whatever order you would decide, it is your own personal meaning, constructed from the phrases given. In music, if there were 'right' answers, there would only be one recording of most major works. However, as there are many recordings, we know that this is because there are numerous interpretations – some of which we will personally prefer to others. Whatever your selection of patterns, can you say why you have chosen them? Here, you are being asked to explain your personal judgement. This is what is meant by 'appraising'.

> 'Describe, discuss and undertake simple analysis and evaluation of musical compositions and performances.'
> (Taken from Non Statutory Guidelines for Music B3, June 1992, Diagram 1)

Track 19 📼

Finally, listen to a selection of musical sound groups. See if you can match the sounds to the symbolic notation we are using. As they are, they are just sound sources – but how can we structure them?

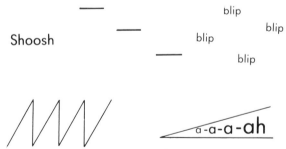

Figure 21 Symbolic notations for sounds

Which sound group could we begin with? Which will be chosen to 'end' the composition? Again, what informs our decisions will, more than likely, be personal preferences or an imagined storyline which these sound groups could be used to portray. Several options follow on the tape.

Which organisational sequence do you like? Why? Do any of the structures conjure up a story-board, or create a picture in your mind?

TAPE: TRACKS 20–24 (DYNAMICS)

Perhaps the previous 'compositions' could be further enhanced with the use of dynamics. This word refers to the degrees of loudness or quietness called for in music. (Remember the opposite of soft is hard, not loud!) Of course, we are not just talking about loud and quiet sounds, but all the degrees of sound in between those two extremes.

Track 20

This track takes one of the previous examples (from Track 18) and applies 'dynamics'. Do you think that this improves the overall 'musical sense' of the composition? Why? What does the addition of this expressive form achieve?

Sometimes, composers indicate their preferences for dynamics on their scores; both words and symbols can be used.

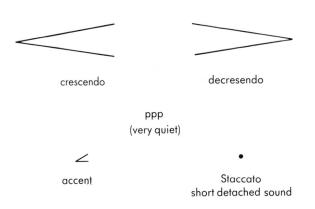

crescendo   decresendo

ppp
(very quiet)

accent   Staccato
short detached sound

Figure 22   Words and symbols for dynamics

A conductor or director will use gestures to show how they would like the sounds to be 'uttered' at a given time.

Figure 23   Using gestures to show how sounds are to be 'uttered'

This may be at the conductor's discretion, or as a reminder to the players of the composer's intentions.

Track 21

To emphasise the structural technique of an 'echo', the use of dynamics is essential to actually highlight the feature of the echo. First, listen to 'Frère Jacque' without dynamics, and then played with dynamics. You will no doubt agree that the 'dynamics' highlight the echo form.

Track 22

Dynamics also contribute to musical meaning in other ways. In the track 'Train is a-coming' you will hear the journey of the train, at first in the distance and then arriving at the station, before departing and moving off into the distance once more.

Track 23 📼

The subtleties of gradation in volume can be extremely powerful in evoking the listener's emotions. Listen to these two extracts, and reflect on the feelings the music seems to evoke in you or, indeed, the imagery the sounds generate.

Track 24 📼

The other aspect of this element referred to in the National Curriculum is that of accent, or the stressing of certain sounds. We encountered this a little at the start of the tape. Sometimes the first beat of a bar may be given slightly more stress (remember the waltz: 1–2–3–1–2–3–1–2–3, etc.). Again, accent, or stress, is used to create special effects, selected with the intention of causing an effect on the listener. Try clapping out the pattern below, placing a stress in your clapping where you see (>).

Did you find that the stress or accent did not come where you felt it should? Did this, perhaps, catch you off guard? There was certainly nothing regular or reliable about the accents. This leaves us on edge, as there is nothing predictable about the 'organised patterns of sound' we hear.

Listen to this excerpt from Stravinsky's 'Rite of Spring: Dance of the Adolescents'. What feelings did the composer's use of accent evoke for you?

Our version was prepared on computer. You might like to listen to an orchestral recording of this work to hear not only the differences and similarities, but also the context into which this extract fits.

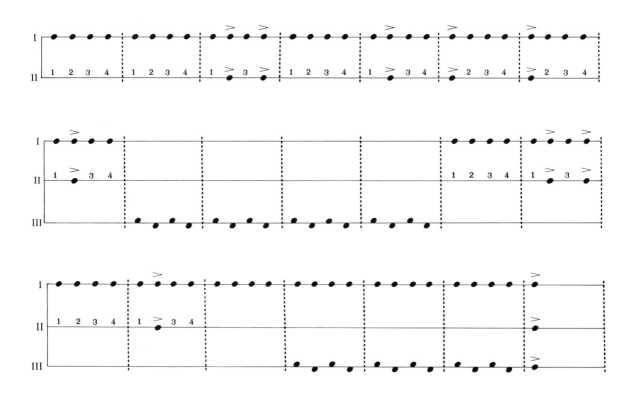

Figure 24 Clap out the pattern (Stravinsky)

TAPE: TRACKS 25–29 (PACE/TEMPO)

Another expressive technique used in the composition of music is that of pace or tempo. This refers to the speed of a piece of music and/or the subtle speed changes that may occur during a composition.

Track 25

We all know what happens if someone tries to play or sing our favourite hymn or folk tune too fast. Somehow the emotional impact the song has for us is severely reduced.

Track 26

If the tempo does not allow for the clear articulation of words, meaning can be lost altogether in a song, as we can hear on this track. Variations in speed can also add to the dramatic effect of the music, or reinforce the meanings conveyed with words or melody line. Note the

'pause' symbol up above the word 'sky' and 'go'. This means that the performers can pause or wait on this note for longer than the note-value actually written (which is two beats). The word 'rallentando' which appears over the last bar is Italian for 'hold back, gradually get slower'.

In the second version of this children's action song, hear how changes in tempo encourage fuller access to the song. Which version do you prefer? Could you say why?

Track 27

Tempo or pace can also be important for other reasons. Some instruments lend themselves to short, rapid sounds more readily than others – I have in mind the beloved classroom triangle, which small hands certainly cannot manage at great speeds, whereas claves or maracas pose fewer problems if the pace of the composition is increased.

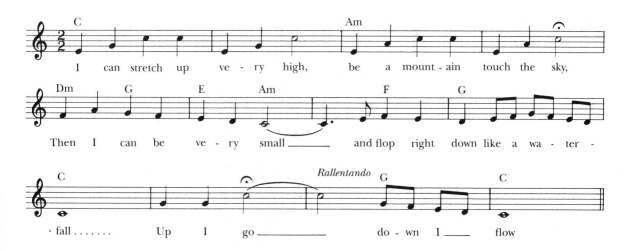

Figure 25 Notation for 'I Can Stretch' written by d'Reen Struthers © 1989 Inter-Action

Track 28

The focus when listening to Track 22 was dynamics. The same track is repeated here but, this time, listen out for the gradual changes in tempo which match the lyrics about the journey of the train. This is an obvious use of tempo to highlight meaning. Can you think of other situations or emotional moments where speed may be relevant? What about walking in the dark, or the gradual onset of fear or excitement? If we have done our own 'brainstorming' of ideas, our questioning of pupils could be more purposeful and flexible – certainly the way we are able to respond to their compositions will be enhanced if we have a repertoire of options to offer them for developing or extending the expressive qualities of their musical utterances.

Track 29

Take, for example, this track. Composed in the style of a march, hear what happens when the conductor or director sets off at the wrong speed. The same piece is repeated at what could be considered a more appropriate speed.

TAPE: TRACKS 30–34 (TIMBRE)

This term refers to the 'quality of the sound'. This may be differentiated in numerous ways. Each track that follows will highlight a different area.

Track 30

First, we have the sound qualities of different instruments, as a result of their physical properties or characteristics, for example, wooden, metal, plastic, ceramic, natural fibres (skin, gut) and size of sound box or vibrating chamber. You will hear four sounds on this track. From the pictures below, can you match the sounds to the instruments? (Notice five sound sources have been drawn.) Answers on p. 49.

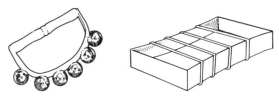

Figure 26 Match the sounds to the instruments

Track 31

Listen to these same sounds, this time labelling the sounds by the way they are played (for example, tapped, plucked, blown, scraped, shaken, bowed).

Figure 27 Record your results in the table

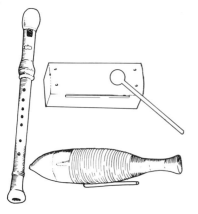

SOUNDS HEARD	PHYSICAL PROPERTIES (TRACK 30)	HOW SOUNDS WERE MADE (TRACK 31)
1		
2		
3		
4		

Track 32

What we have been doing is grouping the sounds into families or 'sets', first, by the way the sounds originated and, secondly, by the way in which they were generated. This is where we also get the categories found in the Western orchestra – string, woodwind, brass and percussion. The timbral qualities of each group are quite unique. On this track, you will hear three versions of the same piece, 'In the Darkness', each version played by a different 'family' of instruments. You might have a preference for one tone colour, and yet feel that it does not suit the particular musical example I have selected. Answers on p. 49.

Track 33

'In the Darkness' was inspired by childhood memories of lying in bed and watching the beam of light as a torch is shone around a room. The rhythmic pattern and pulse I chose was intended to create the effect of long, slow gestures with the torch beam – not short, sharp, jerky ones. Therefore, to create this 'feel', the most appropriate instruments will be those that can make long, slow sounds. The wood block and other such percussion instruments would not be appropriate for the 'feeling' I was trying to create.

First, you will hear a plucked violin playing the melody line while I sing, and then the violin will be bowed. List other instruments which could also have been selected to give this long, smooth feel. Answers on p. 49.

Often, the way an instrument is played can affect the tone. Try playing the same note on a xylophone – how many different sound-colours can be created?

Figure 29   Playing the xylophone

Track 34

Voices have very different tone-colours or timbres. Babies can distinguish the familiar voice timbres from about three months. Sometimes, we will want to use these differences to create desired

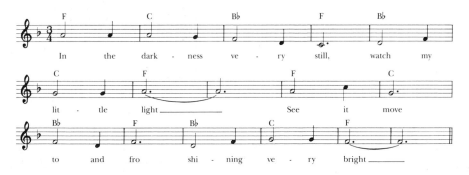

Figure 28   'In The Darkness' written by d'Reen Struthers © 1989 Inter-Action

effects. We may select the 'soprano', or very high register, for the voice of the bird and the 'bass', or lowest register, for the voice of the elephant. Such registers can be found in most musical sets – from the steel drum family, to the sections of the Western orchestra, and the gamelan of the south-east Asian orchestra. There are scientific justifications for these sound registers. The length of the string or tube or the size of the sound box all affect the quality of the sound made. Saint-Saëns carefully selected the instruments for his 'elephants' and 'hens' from 'Carnival of the Animals'. Track 34 was inspired by this composer. You may like to listen to his version and consider the similarities and differences.

TAPE: TRACKS 35–42 (PITCH)

Track 35 ▭

You will hear 'father bear' talking in his deep, low voice. In contrast, now listen to baby bear with his squeaky, light, high voice. (Played twice.)

Figure 30 Bear talk

Track 36 ▭

Now beginning with father bear down low, you will now hear mother bear whose voice is neither that low or as high as baby bear's. Her voice is **in-between**. Finally, you will hear again baby bear. (The sequence is now reversed: baby bear, mother bear, father bear.)

Track 37 ▭

The order has now been changed. Hear baby bear on the violin, then father bear on double-bass followed by mother bear on cello. (Played twice.)

Track 38 ▭

This sequence – high, low, in-between – is found in a nursery rhyme. Listen to the bear sequence from the string section, and then the first two phrases of 'Hot cross buns'. Trace the sounds you hear with the aid of this diagram.

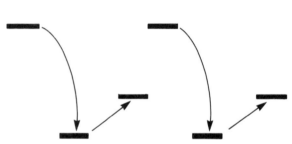

Figure 31 Trace the sound shapes

Track 39 ▭

Such sounds move in many ways. We have been 'leaping' from high to low to in-between in the examples heard so far. Listen again to the first two phrases of 'Hot cross buns'. Listen next to the third phrase of our nursery rhyme, 'One-a-penny, two-a-penny'. Here the movement of the notes is

Figure 32 Visual representation of notes in steps

in steps: first going down (**getting lower**) and then going up (**getting higher**). (See also figure 32 opposite.) (Played twice.)

Track 40 📼

Together we now have the melody line of the nursery rhyme. You may like to draw the shape of the melody in the air as you hear it on the tape. (Pupils find gestures and such visual clues helpful also.)

Track 41 📼

Sometimes the movements may be very small. If we play this white note (as indicated by number '1' on the keyboard) and then move up to the black note, we have travelled half a tone.

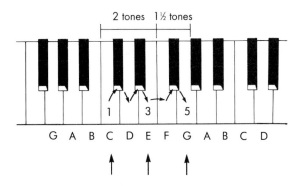

Figure 33 Between 1 and 3 on the keyboard there are two whole tones

If we continue up on to the next white note, that is another half tone again. Indeed, to get then from the white note marked (1) to the white note marked (3), we have travelled two whole complete tones, and then one and a half tones to get to the white note marked (5). This becomes exciting when we play three notes ascending in a particular 'stride' pattern. First, hear the notes played separately and then hear them played together as a **chord**. This is a 'happy' or major chord. The notes you hear can also be called 'doh–me–soh'. (Like the start of the song '*Michael row* the boat ashore'.) By changing the

interval between the first and second notes of our chord, we can create a 'sad' or minor chord. The distances travelled then become:

C (2 tones) **E** (1½ tones) **G** – Major scale

C (1½ tones) **E** flat (2 tones) **G** – Minor scale

You will see that this sequence can be repeated elsewhere on the keyboard as there are repeated patterns – notice that the black keys are laid out in sets of two and three, that is, as black twins and black triplets.

Let us return to our nursery rhyme 'Hot cross buns'. What role can a chord play in this song? On the music printed below, notice there are two letters, C and F, which are printed above the 'stave' (the name for the five lines and four spaces). These are an indication of the chords (guitar, auto-harp, chime-bar group) which can be played.

Figure 34 The chords in 'Hot cross buns'

On the tape you will hear, first the journey described up the keyboard, matching the description given in the text, and including the vocal form of 'Michael Row' and 'doh – me – soh'. Finally you will hear, the C chord played as single notes then together. The song is then sung with the chord being played underneath on the first beat of each bar. Listen for the clash that sometimes seems to occur, especially on 'buns' and 'two-a-penny'. Listen to this discordant sound played again, and then hear how it is solved by playing the second chord (F) as indicated above the stave. Maybe you will hear also that it is much easier for the singer to make sense of the 'melody' line when the appropriate chords are played. Within Key Stage 2, pupils are expected to be introduced to the elements of 'melody' and 'chords'.

Track 42 📼

Sounds may also move in 'strides' (covering several steps together), as in playing out the chord. In this extract, you will hear the melody line moving upwards in strides and returning

downwards in steps. This diagram may help:

FOUR BIG STEPS UP, FIVE LITTLE STEPS DOWN

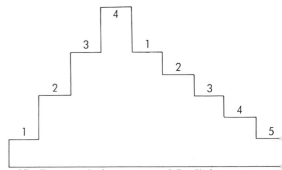

Figure 35 Four musical steps up and five little steps down

TAPE: TRACKS 43–47 (TEXTURE)

Having journeyed through the 'musical elements', I shall now consider 'texture' (defined by the Working Party as 'the result of combining or interrelating parts in music. Many parts create a denser texture than do a few parts' (DES, 1991)). Put another way, imagine one solo voice singing a tune and then imagine the same tune accompanied by a rich backing of voices and/or instruments. The texture of both would be very different.

Track 43 📼

First, you will hear two melodic sentences (made up of four phrases), followed (on the next track) by the same sentence performed with a full orchestral backing.

Figure 36 Score of phrases

Track 44 📼

The example is our own mini concerto for flute and orchestra. The voices in the orchestra all have their own melodic line and are rhythmically independent. This is called 'polyphony'. The texture could certainly be described as more dense than the first example!

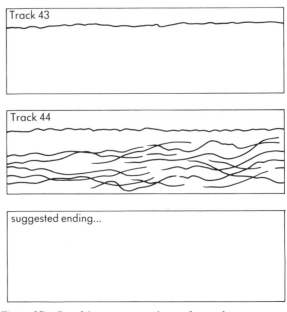

Figure 37 Graphic representations of sound

This piece has not been finished. What do you think the orchestra could do next? You may like to fill in the empty box with your suggestion. Certainly pupils will enjoy this type of encouragement.

Track 45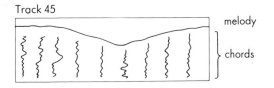

We return to a previous example, 'I can stretch'. Listen to the melody line with an accompaniment made by a simple chord progression and compare this diagram with the ones for Tracks 43 and 44.

Figure 38   Graphic representations of sound

Track 46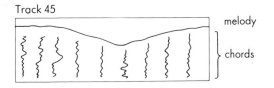

The combinations of different types of instruments from different pitch registers creates a unique texture. On this track, listen out for the

very high sounds combined with the very low sounding instruments. The texture is rather like a holey jumper. Does it have the effect of leaving you feeling a bit tense and cold?

Track 47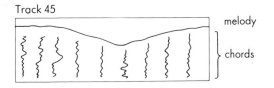

In contrast, listen to the warmer, closer texture of this madrigal entitled 'Silver Swan', written in 1612 by Orlando Gibbons, where the numerous voices are all talking in close harmony together (another form of polyphony). Compare these diagrams for Tracks 46 and 47 with those presented earlier. Is there any similarity?

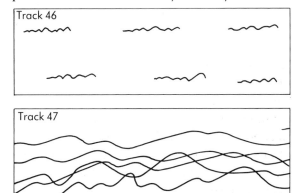

Figure 39   Graphic representations of sound

COMMENT

The National Curriculum Council describes the 'elements' as 'the "building blocks" of music – as an artist uses colour, texture, line and shape, a composer will use the elements of pitch, dynamics, duration, timbre, texture and structure'. As we have seen, the way musical elements are combined and organised can completely change the 'feel' of the sounds heard.

If we are going to encourage children to engage in musical experiences, then our knowledge of what the constituent parts are is vital. But we must also begin to think openly

about these possibilities. What would happen if we changed the instruments? Would the expressive qualities change? Why did the composer shape the melody line in that way? Indeed, the questions asked so far are exactly the kinds of questions that can be asked of younger listeners. This is because we not only want to ensure that they have the opportunity to 'listen to music', but that in the process 'their ears are working'! As we engage children purposefully in musical experiences, they will be developing a growing repertoire of musical thoughts and ideas.

This bank of musical possibilities can then be called upon as they are encouraged to make musical decisions in their own compositions and performances.

SOUND AND SYMBOL MATCHING

As we have seen, sound can be represented in numerous ways, depending on the meaning that we confer to symbols. I have shown children as young as three and a half to five years cards with the following symbols:

Figure 40   Card symbols

and have made 'mouth noises', for example, 'pisst bit bit pisst', asking them if I am making the sounds on the card. Immediately, they appear to recognise that there is a mismatch sound-to-symbol, and say 'no'. I then ask them to read and make the sounds that are on the card. They reply with 'pisst pisst bit pisst' (Track 48). Of course, they are learning at this moment to make a sound-to-symbol match. They have recognised that the visual pattern does not match the sound pattern. In this instance, as the visual pattern is clearly not for changing, the variable is the voice which can be altered to more 'appropriately' match the symbol.

Here, the children are developing the pre-reading skill of following a line from left to right, and connecting a symbol with a sound utterance. I had not noticed that a child had left the group, gone to the painting corner and was producing her own line of symbols. Mariam returned joyously waving her composition for us all to see. I asked her to 'play' her pattern, which she did with much pride. I then asked the class if they could play this pattern on their bodies. Selecting Turlin, he clapped and stamped to match the two shapes

Mariam had used in her painting. When turned upside down the symbols suggest other vocal/body sounds.

Figure 41   Mariam's notation

The next step, in a different lesson, would have been to have the children develop this sound-to-symbol match using instruments. I could have watched them 'controlling' their instruments, as well as organising themselves as they sequenced the patterns they had created.

This sound-to-symbol match is important not just for 'making' musical sounds. It is also an important aspect of developing the inner ear. While looking at a visual cue, can the children hear the sounds in their heads? Let us consider some simple cartoons:

Figure 42 Visual cues – long sounds and short sounds
Inspired by Upbeat, Bojangles Music, 1984, Australia

This instance involved registering the picture and locating a copy of the sound from your mind's memory banks. A different challenge could be set by changing the caption below to read: Which things have a steady beat or have no beat?

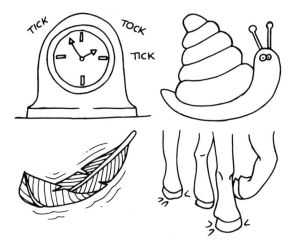

Figure 43 Visual cues – beat or no beat
Inspired by Upbeat, Bojangles Music, 1984, Australia

This again engages us in matching sounds from our own memory banks to those in the pictures.

Something we often get young children to do is to match the picture to the word. What would happen if the word was not written with letters, but presented in syllabification boxes?

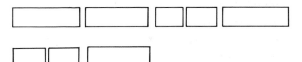

Figure 44 Visual cues – syllabification or rhythmic patterns
Inspired by Upbeat, Bojangles Music, 1984, Australia

To match the picture to the box, it is necessary to say the words in our head (or out loud), but we need to hear its rhythmic pattern – a development from clapping one's own name. With this we have shown that a word, standing for an object, can be represented in another way. This is an important aspect of visual/aural matching in musical contexts. With an older age group, such an exercise might look like this: 'Draw a line from the word-phrase to the pattern matching it:'

Happy, happy, happy days   — — — — — — — ——

Clap, clap, clap your hands   —— —— —— — ——

Ticka tocka ticka tocka   —— —— — — ——

Skip, skip skip to my lou   — — — — — — — —

Figure 45   Word phrase patterns

It is often said of 'music' that it is one of the subjects that **all** pupils can readily have access to. Certainly, if no hearing impediment exists, this should be true. However, if the teacher begins a dialogue with the class about the sounds heard, those children who do not feel confident with English as their first language are often excluded. If, on the other hand, we offer some visual prompts, those same children can become engaged by signalling their comprehension of the sounds heard, using visual representations to indicate the qualities of the sounds, the sequence of sounds heard, etc.

Arising from this line of thinking, it then follows that with this approach, young children will have begun not only to value the role of symbols, but can also be encouraged to devise symbols, signs and graphics which accurately capture the quality of sounds they make. Indeed, as with the actual sounds they make, in our capacity as 'mediators', we should always be attempting to enhance the quality of the pupils' musical experiences. The transcribing of their compositions should not just be an exercise (as required by the National Curriculum), but a meaningful activity which ensures that the composers, or others, would be able to 'read' and translate the 'notation' into similar sounds on another occasion. Therefore, representation of the sounds needs to include indications of the expressive qualities of the sound. This can be done either by using separate symbols for both the sounds and the expressive qualities, or by combining the two aspects in one form of representation.

The 1994 Draft Proposals for the Music National Curriculum state:

From the Key stage-specific Programme of study for KS1:
   *'Pupils should be **taught** to:*
   a) sing songs from memory and perform short musical patterns by ear and from symbols;

d) rehearse and share their music making;
h) record their composition using symbols where appropriate, and communicate simple musical ideas to others.'
And within the End of Key Stage Statement (KS1):
'. . . They should relate symbols to sounds and sounds to symbols.'

From the Key stage-specific Programme of study for KS2:

   'Pupils should be **taught** *to:*

a) sing songs from memory and perform musical patterns of increasing length from ear and from notation(s), *e.g. symbols which define pitch, timbre, duration;*

d) rehearse direct and present their own projects/performances;

h) review and refine their compositions and communicate musical ideas to others, using notation(s).'

And within the End of Key Stage Statement (KS2):
'. . . use notation(s).'

SCAA 1994

TAPE: TRACKS 48–65
(NOTATIONS – SOUND-TO-SYMBOL MATCHING)

Matched to audio tracks on the tape, the following symbolic forms of sound demonstrate some of the possibilities with which children may wish to work. Note that listening to the recording of the actual sounds also requires a recognition of their expressive qualities and the contextual structure in which they are found. Having already been introduced to the musical elements (beat, rhythm, structure, dynamics, tempo, timbre, pitch, texture) you will find it rewarding to keep these in mind as you follow the examples below. A selection of various possibilities is given, matched to sound tracks. There is no significance in the order in which these examples have been presented.

For all of the following tracks (48–65) I suggest that you read the text accompanying each track first and then use the diagrams as you listen.

Track 48 📼

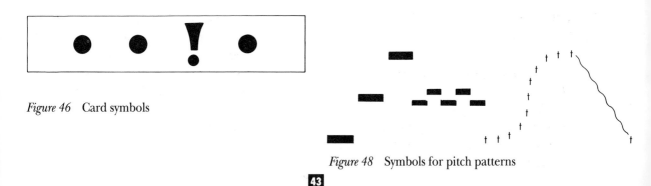

Figure 46 Card symbols

Track 49 📼

The notion of 'bold' can also be found in computer/IT language. In this context, it is used to imply an emphasis, a bold or loud sound, as opposed to the lighter sound in the contrasting example.

Figure 47 Symbols for loud and quiet sound

Track 50 📼

On this track, notice how the ascending sounds in the first section are longer in comparison to those sounds in the second, as mirrored in the size of the shapes. Hear also how the direction of the second group does not move in strides as in the first. By contrast, the third section shows how the composer would like the 't's' to travel, marking out both direction and manner.

Figure 48 Symbols for pitch patterns

Track 51 📼

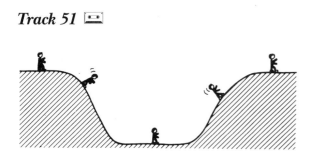

Figure 49 A 'musical' journey

This cartoon clearly illustrates a 'journey' which involves physical movement. There are possibilities for pupils to make this journey demonstrating, first, their understanding of the speed/tempo involved and, secondly, their control over an instrument to show those gradual tempo changes in sound. Placed on a sound table, such illustrations can be very useful to prompt focused articulation of sound to match a visual sequence. (See figure 50 opposite.)

Track 52 📼

Four examples demonstrating still more ways of representing pitch. All but one also include suggestions for expressive qualities.

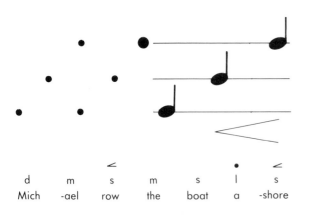

Figure 51 Ways of representing pitch

Figure 50 Pupil group playing from a cartoon strip

Track 53 📼

Young children are encouraged to recite numbers in sequence. But this is not just a row of numbers!

What can we notice? What could these marks mean in a musical context? How shall we respond to the marks we find? First pattern A, followed by pattern B and then the two together played through twice.

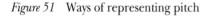

Figure 52 Numbers, pulse and rhythm

The sounds made from this sequence could look like this written in musical rhythmic notation:

Figure 53   Musical rhythmic notation

Grids

Track 54 📼

Young children may not be able to draw the instruments. When diagrams of the instruments are photocopied and put on to small cards, the children can structure and sequence a 'composition' which can then be played. In pairs, with the musical score boards hidden from view, the listener could try to 'write' what they heard, by selecting and ordering further pictures. Both sets of scores are then 'exposed' and can be matched.

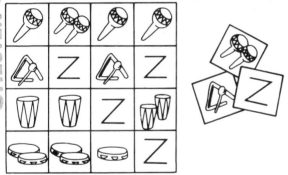

Figure 54   Children can 'write' musical scores using picture cards

This could be expanded by playing all or some parts together. One instrument is missing when they all play together. Can you identify which one?

Track 55 📼

A more sophisticated version of Track 54. The pictures are replaced with sound patterns (which could be thought of as 'tea' and 'coffee'). Each child who thinks he/she has a wooden instrument plays line one, and then waits and listens while

the other instruments play their respective lines. The wooden instrument players should then be ready to come in again after the drum line.

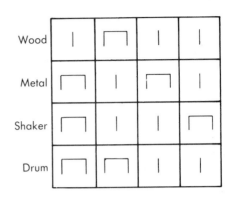

Figure 55   Grid with standard rhythmic notation

How to begin? Who will count the group in? What will they count (perhaps an introductory one, two, three, four to come in, as deductable from the four boxes across the grid)? What about the tempo? What do the players notice as they listen to the other lines playing? Can they hear the differences in timbre (the tone colour of the other instruments)? How could the playing be improved? All players need to 'think' and 'listen'. Saying the words of the rhythmic pattern in your head also helps to improve the coherence of the performance! (The grid is played through four times altogether.)

Track 56 📼

The grid pattern from the previous example can be played to any music which has a 'four-beat' feel to it. Naturally, some music may feel more appropriate than others. First, you will hear an accompaniment I have chosen, which includes an introduction and a voice-over counting in. Try playing along yourself. Next, you will hear the grid from Track 55, played with the accompanying music. This whole activity could be extended, once the players are confident, to take account of changes in dynamics.

Track 57

We now extend the use of the grid to include 'pitch'. Using the same rhythmic sequence as in Track 55, indications of high or low are shown with the letters 'H' and 'L'.

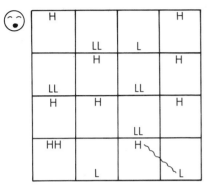

Figure 56 Grid with pitch symbols

First, you will hear this and then a group of children providing a percussion pulse or beat. You will hear how one, using a wooden agogo, gradually realises that his instruments can play two different sounds and that he can represent the grid indications on his instruments. What other possibilities are there?

Track 58

Describing sounds with words and pictures.

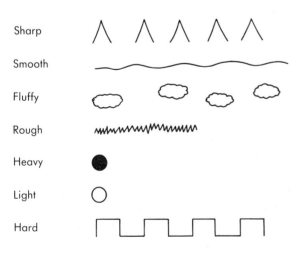

Figure 57 Words represented by symbols and sounds

Listen to our vocal suggestions – on the next track some have been used in a composition.

Track 59

A composition using these sounds.

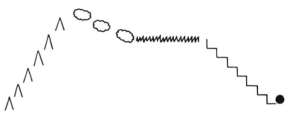

Figure 58 Composition made using the sound symbols

Track 60

Visual clues can be useful to show what can be heard in the music. On this track, you will hear three short sound-pictures to match these pictures.

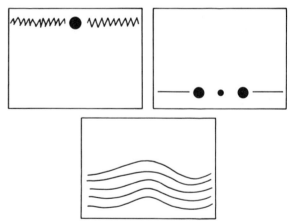

Figure 59 Visual clues

Track 61

On this track, a combination of classroom, computer and vocal sounds can be heard to represent the pictures, which could be given names such as 'night-time' and 'rain'.

Figure 60 Visual pictures for texture

Track 62 📼

Scores can take many different forms.

Figure 61 Different scores

Track 63 📼

Telephones alive (pitch patterns in sequence).

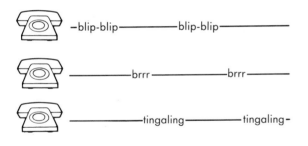

Figure 62 Pitch patterns – telephones

Track 64 📼

The trio for instruments.

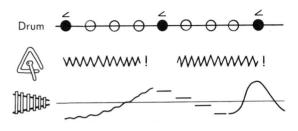

Figure 63 Graphic notation

To ensure players are all using the same pulse, some cue system for beginning is necessary. This could be a conductor, someone verbally counting in, or a short pattern which signals the pulse and the entry point. You will hear such a pattern at the start of this track.

Track 65 📼

There are many ways to indicate accompaniments to songs: 'In the darkness'.

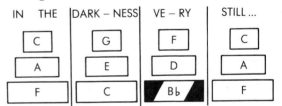

Figure 64 Ways of illustrating accompaniments to songs

SUMMARY

Investigating music involves more than just detective work. At the same time as we are gaining an understanding of what the actual building materials are, we are also perceiving the materials in combination. The effect that a low, slow, long bowed sound pattern has will most likely be very different to that of a much higher, shorter, more jerky whistle-like sound played on the recorder or piccolo. How is this possible? At the moment where we move away from merely describing the properties of a phenomenon, whether it is music, a flower or another human being, we begin instead to actually 'experience' that phenomenon. Our perception of these properties has to relate to our own experiential world if the music is to be humanly significant. One way we achieve this is through the use of our imagination. This is a natural, creative process which we enjoy from early childhood when we learn by projecting ourselves into all kinds of imaginary worlds. These worlds not only have different scenery, but while in them, we can actually 'feel' different feelings and see ourselves behaving and responding in different ways. It is important, therefore, that when we begin to 'investigate music' with children, that we constantly affirm the expressive qualities and always seek to ask questions which sharpen their perception and heighten their awareness.

By way of a conclusion to this chapter, the two points Charles Leonhard, Professor of Music at the University of Illinois, made in 1982 still remain true. He said:

> 'The strength of music as an art and the reason every society has nurtured and valued its music lie in the strong appeal of music to the life of feeling and to the imagination.'

Secondly, he gives a warning:

> 'In children's early years and, perhaps even in kindergarten, music is a source of delight, an avenue for self-expression, a spur to the imagination and a high level of feeling. As children move through successive years, however, they find less and less in school music to feel good about and more and more to learn about it; much of what they are expected to learn has little or nothing to do with the enchantment they found in music originally.' (Leonhard, 1982)

Having thus investigated the nature of the 'sound phenomenon' (one of the crucial components in our challenge diagram), we continue our journey. In Chapter 3 we shall be looking more closely at the learner – the pupil (human phenomenon) and the development of musical processes.

SUGGESTIONS

1   Listen to your favourite piece of music. Make a mental note of what it is about how the musical materials have been organised that informs your love of the track.

2   Can the same performance be musically rewarding for the performer and unrewarding for the audience, or vice versa? Why or why not?

3   Select a listening example with which you are unfamiliar. On your first hearing, note down what general feelings the piece left you with and/or what imagery if provoked. On the second hearing, take particular note of what it was in the music that could have made you feel or imagine these things; how were the elements used in combination? With the third hearing, focus even further on those elements and try to define their specific properties. Make notes on each process.

4   Discuss the implications of musical meaning as distinct from musical content. To what extent may music educators be placing too great an emphasis on the content of music rather than on the meanings inherent in the musical experience? What would be some of the educational implications if the process were to be reversed?

ANSWERS TO EXERCISES

Track 2

TRACK	№ OF BEATS	
2 a	1234	reggae
b	123	waltz
c	1234	march
d	1234/12	jazz

Track 9

TRACK	LONG	SHORT	INSTRUMENT	
9 1	✓		b	gazoo
2		✓	c	claves
3		✓	a	drum
4	✓		e	shaker

Track 10

The second example did not use 'marching-band-type instruments' for example, there were plucked string instruments rather than the usual brass instruments. The music appears to stumble, as it is a bit too slow to march along to. (You might like to see what your pupils make of these two examples.)

Tracks 30 and 31

SOUNDS HEARD	PHYSICAL PROPERTIES (TRACK 30)	HOW SOUNDS WERE MADE (TRACK 31)
1	wooden/plastic	blown
2	wooden	tapped
3	metal	shaken
4	wooden	scraped

Track 32

Order of instruments heard on the tape: strings – brass – percussion.

Track 33

Other instruments which might give a long smooth accompaniment for the song 'In the darkness' could include: strings (bowed) and wind instruments (brass or woodwind).

THREE

Acknowledging the learner

This book regards the teacher as a mediator. The challenge is therefore to mediate between the sound phenomenon and the human phenomenon. To do this, I believe teachers not only need an understanding of *'musical processes' (see Chapter 2), but they also need to have knowledge of the human phenomenon – the learner.*

WHO ARE THE LEARNERS?

Let us begin by considering the musical experiences many pupils may have already had. It is likely that all your pupils will have encountered 'music' prior to commencing school, as many family homes are now dominated by television. Children will have experienced everything from cartoons to the signature tunes for the news or their big brother's favourite television drama. Many will have aural discriminatory powers (and musical memories) that will enable them to recognise these melodies in different contexts – imagine a salesperson in the local shopping centre, demonstrating the capabilities of the latest electronic keyboard by playing the 'Neighbours' theme tune. Those children who have had a regular 'acquaintance' with the programme may possibly be able to recognise the tune as 'familiar', or go so far as to be able to identify the context, 'Isn't that the theme tune to Nan's favourite programme?' Further, if we asked them to sing the 'tune' of Nan's favourite programme, we would probably find a surprising number of pupils who could. Already, these pupils have acquired skills which could be further developed in the classroom, indeed, would be developed by

the inferred processes underlying the Music National Curriculum.

Already equipped with such skills, a pupil will be fascinated to develop and build on this acquired knowledge in order to extend and apply their musical understanding. As teachers, our planning should, therefore, begin at the point that the pupil has already reached. It is important to first acknowledge and then build on these important skills and capabilities.

This is just as true for the young new arrival as for a pupil entering the junior school and embarking on Key Stage 2. What previous musical experiences have they had? Their musical background may be fuller if they have experienced music in the home environment or in their previous school years. How did these previous experiences build on each other? Maybe they did not! Perhaps the pupil had a limited number of pleasurable musical encounters, like when they were allowed to sing in the choir, some occasional opportunities to play an instrument, and memories of having to sit on a cold wooden floor and listen to 'music' before the head teacher talked to them for what seemed like forever! That is quite a 'collection' of experience! In this scenario, the pupils' emotional engagement with the experiences they have had may not have been rewarding and positively motivating. Sadly, this emotional 'memory' can scar quite deeply and last for a long time, as many adults can testify!

ARE THERE STAGES OF MUSICAL DEVELOPMENT?

Just as there is a great deal of debate about the notion of general 'stages' of child development, we should not be surprised to learn of similar debates in music education circles. Of course, we could be fooled into thinking otherwise. Numerous National Curriculum documents seem to suggest that there are, indeed, developmental stages or phases that pupils pass through – even the terminology of the National Curriculum leads us to this conclusion, such as End of Key Stage Statements. However, as our 'learners' are both thinking and feeling beings, it is hard to comprehend learning existing on merely a lineal plane. All learning is 'provisional' and interactive. We must, therefore, not equate musical learning solely with the acquisition of 'technical skills'. Musical learning is just as much about 'thinking' and 'feeling' as skill acquisition, and some would argue that the technical skills without the 'feeling' would result in a sterile performance.

There are those, however, who have conducted 'research' into such questions as 'Do children register pitch before rhythm?' (Wing, 1948); 'What is musical aptitude?' (Seashore, 1938); 'What is the highest note perceivable?' (Bentley, 1966). While this type of research continues, other research has evolved which has focused on observing children's musical behaviour as composers, performers and listeners in classrooms.

CHILDREN AS PERCEIVERS – LISTENERS AND APPRAISERS

Sound is all around us. It is likely that most of the children we deal with will have arrived at school with varying degrees of linguistic skill in their mother tongue. In other words, most have already begun to discriminate sounds and, more significantly, attribute meaning to the sounds they hear and utter themselves. This meaning will have been occurring within a social/cultural context (Vygotsky, 1934; Bruner, 1966). Consider the toddler's recognition of when their carer is very annoyed. Possibly, they will have observed a change in body language, heard a change in the tone of voice used, and possibly even experienced some physical pain. These changes may have also been observed in other people around them, seen demonstrated by cartoon characters and displayed on television. Hence, it is reasonable to suggest that when similar changes in body gesture and tone of voice are perceived in a classroom context, the pupil may correctly register the meaning of the situation to be similarly one of annoyance or anger.

What of the messages already received about styles of music? Does the young child observe a carer's pleasure in some sounds and not in others? Is the music of an older sibling the cause for tension in the household? What music seems to be associated with harmony, happiness, the child's pleasure? If in the Latin American household, the sound of salsa music conjures up a memory of many happy people, dancing and interacting with the child, there can be little

Figure 65   Choosing the sound or instrument heard

doubt why this youngster is positively inclined towards this style of music. Indeed, the pupil would probably have little difficulty in saying why they liked salsa. Their appraisal, however, would not be based on musical understandings, but on context. As teachers, we work within educational contexts. This surely means that we should be considering ways of linking people with their experiences in such ways as to help make those and future experiences more meaningful and valuable.

Consider what happens in 'early years' education. We encourage children to begin to make sense of the world, by categorising and naming 'sets' (of shapes, number, objects, colours). Why not do this with sound? Have the children group the instruments

- by the way sounds can be made (shaking, blowing, tapping, scraping, etc.);
- by the sounds themselves (long, short, high, low, wooden, metal, human, etc. (See Chapter 2 pp. 22 and 34.)

Asking them to discriminate between different sounds played on a tape-recorder or from behind a screen is actually asking the learner to demonstrate numerous things. First, can they recognise that two sounds are different? Secondly, can they identify what was the cause of the difference? The answer may be as vague as 'because there were different instruments' or as specific as 'one sound was made by a drum and the other by rattling your keys'. Of course, those children who do not have the vocabulary to name the objects will not be excluded from the discussion, if you provide visual representations of the 'sound makers'. (Indeed, it provides a good motivational context where it becomes meaningful for the vocabulary to be acquired.)

In this manner, we are able to ascertain whether the pupils' 'ears are working'! Are some children unable to perceive the differences or similarities, for instance, between sounds blown or produced by tapping, despite similar pitches or timbre? This may, of course, mean that they have not previously had an opportunity to investigate these ranges of sound-producers, either at home or in another setting. We may be asking them to respond to a task for which they have no previous repertoire of knowledge upon which to draw.

Now, the significance of relating our understanding of 'educational psychology' to a musical context will be apparent. We cannot expect the young learner to demonstrate their understanding of something, or to apply this understanding to a problem set, or a new context created, unless we have offered ground work. Naturally, there will be some children who will show greater 'aptitude' in certain areas. They may be quicker than others at making the discriminatory judgements you are expecting. They may appear inhibited in their responses to isolated 'sound' examples (maybe they have not had the opportunity to play many sound games?), while being alert to *distinguishing* the sounds from within a group of sounds. How could this be? If we were to hypothesise about what the answer might be, we would find our focus is sharpened back on to the individual. In this way, we are reminded that the child's emotional engagement in the experience is significant and that this can be influenced by others – at home and at school.

The musical materials investigated in Chapter 2 were all, we discovered, interactive with each other, and the many relationships were imbued with meaning and feelings. Upon perceiving a certain combination or interaction of sound materials, particular imagery was likely to be conjured up. The reverse is also possible – imagery can similarly conjure up or prompt the hearing of imagined sound, perceived by what has been termed the 'inner ear'. Both of these processes are vital to musical development. Both are about perception – external and internal (Chapter 2, p. 39). Indeed, Glover, Curwen and Kodaly were all interested in developing the power of the inner ear through their vocal work.

Within the National Curriculum, reference is also made about the 'internalisation' of sounds:

Key Stage 1 Introductory Statement: '... Pupils should be taught to listen with concentration, by exploring, recognising and internalising, *e.g. hearing in their head*.' Key Stage 2 Introductory Statement: '... Pupils should be taught to listen with attention to detail and identify musical ideas by investigating, distinguishing and internalising the musical elements.' This 'thinking the sound in one's own head' is a skill that many instrumentalists sadly lack, needing their instrument to play the sound before they can hear how the tune sounds.

Perceiving the sound 'internally' is also a necessity when playing by ear. In this process, one is seeking to match the external sounds made with those heard in one's head. In other words, if I am able to sing 'Bye bye Miss American Pie' in my head, I will be able to pick the tune out on an instrument as I simultaneously master the techniques to make the sound. Without the reference of the tune stored in my mind, the process of deciphering would be much slower. It is also a facility that enables us to correct errors. If we have a 'version' stored in our minds (aural memory), anything that does not come close to matching that will be perceived as a different tune altogether. Practice obviously improves our abilities in this area. With this skill in place, the powers to further discriminate variations in dynamics, structure, texture, timbre, tempo and duration are enhanced. The more heightened the skill, the greater the possibilities in other areas of musical development.

Our young learners, therefore, bring to the classroom a range of aural skills and an already acquired collection of perceived aural sounds which may or may not have been classified, organised or registered at a conscious level. As teachers, we can ensure that these previous experiences do not go unacknowledged. Such skills, if practised, developed and extended, will enhance the learner's capacity to engage more meaningfully with sounds in general, and music in particular.

CHILDREN AS CREATORS – IMPROVISERS AND COMPOSERS

As a result of the perceptions discussed above, most children will have begun to 'play with' or manipulate sounds and meaning from an early age, discovering in the process ways of interpreting sounds, signs and, later, the symbols generally used to represent them.

As research in this field reveals, abilities and skills vary tremendously. There seems little consensus about the findings (Swanwick and Tillman, 1986). However, if we consider a child's development as a creator in the field of language and play, there could be processes to inform our deliberations. The notions of 'play' (Bruce, 1987, 1990; Child, 1985; Garvey, 1977) and 'language' are topics in their own right, and are dealt with at considerable length by other writers; I shall only be drawing on selected aspects.

Let me begin with the notion that 'play is always structured by the materials that the participants have available to them' (Moyles, 1989). If it is dry sand, it will be difficult to make pies that retain their shape, and with only your hands and no other containers, the kind of 'play' possible is limited. Similarly, if you have lots of different musical instruments available in the music corner for young children, how will they ever begin to explore the numerous qualities and possibilities of just one? As teachers, one of the most difficult tasks is that of distinguishing between 'play' and 'play behaviours'. For Lewis (1982), 'play' is seen as being internal, affective and natural, while 'play behaviour' is what is manifested by the child or the adult outwardly. This reminds us that, just as perception can be both internal and external, so too can one's ability to play. Play in this latter description could be considered as process, whereas play in the former might conceivably be seen as a mode.

'For the main characteristic of play – whether of child or adult – is not its content but its mode. Play is an approach to action, not a form of activity.'
Bruner (1977, p. v)

Musical 'play' involves the very same approach, although the 'materials' – sounds and their patterns – are not sand or water! Processes, such as investigating, discovering, experimenting, repeating and deviating, selecting and sequencing, are all apparent when watching children play with the materials of music. Have you ever observed the younger child lining up a range of different cars or animals and attempting to change the sound for each 'toy' in his or her line? Not every animal is a 'Moooo', nor is every car a 'brrroooom'. Change the line-up, and the sounds made also change (this is the beginning of a visual representation of sound – a form of notation almost). You may have observed children going through a selection process – picking up each available instrument and discovering what sounds can be heard. After some time, a few seem to have been revisited more frequently. This elimination process leaves any observant carer in little doubt that 'Oh, Jasvinder just loves the triangle – it is her favourite instrument'. But if we watch and listen further, we might see how she begins to form patterns. First, she strikes the triangle and then searches for another instrument to play with the beater she is holding. On discovering a satisfactory sound – the ring made by tapping the chime bar – she seems to begin again, first tapping the triangle, then the chime bar, and then returning to the triangle. With great smiles, we note that the process of investigation continues. Jasvinder finds that not all instruments tapped with the 'silver stick' make a nice sound. So she has, first, made a sequence thus: triangle, chimebar, triangle, cymbal, triangle, Indian bells, triangle, hanging tubes, triangle.

Track 66

(Try imagining the sounds in your head as you follow her sequence or listen to Track 66.)

Figure 66 Jasvinder experimenting with sounds

Pausing for a moment, we could ask, 'Is anything the same about these instruments, or about the sounds they make?' As the observer, we could either ask the child what discoveries have been made, or we could ask ourselves, 'What has the child actually been thinking about, sorting out, actually doing here?' Our job as an observer becomes one of deduction. As adults we have a repertoire of ideas and possibilities based on our own previous understandings and discoveries, and have a greater chance to make more logical connections and deductions. We will notice that all the instruments are made of metal and, when tapped, all produce a long, although each uniquely different, ringing sound. We also notice that a pattern has emerged, Jasvinder punctuating her 'musical sentence or utterance' with a return to the triangle.

With this bank of understanding, our learner is ready to further develop her musical experience.

Could she revisit this? Can she remember what she discovered? Does she have to go through the whole discovery process again to assist her recall? What does it mean if this child can return to the music corner and immediately repeat the sequence she had 'composed' at the previous session?

Her aural memory has managed to retain the order of the sounds along with other information – possibly the shape of the instruments (a visual image memory), the sensations of reaching across the music table to tap the chime bar, or maybe a storyline which she had invented to add meaning to her sequence. Could it have been that the quality of the metal sounds attracted her, as they were reminiscent of the bells heard in the Hindu temple? Was she attempting to repeat patterns heard there? Whatever the truth of the case, the skill is one which is already present within the learner and should now be developed and extended. The pupil who has to repeat the whole process is clearly not starting from the same place, and requires different assistance (see Chapter 4).

Some writers have considered the idea of a sequential model of children's musical development (Swanwick and Tillman, 1986), observing children 'composing', analysing countless tapes of children's compositions, or scrutinising their symbolic forms of representing sounds. However, just as our example has shown, children will have different approaches and starting points. Generalisations then become more difficult to make. Others, while considering ways of responding to pupil compositions, have noted some helpful and interesting generalisations (Davies, 1986) across a range of both singing and instrumental activities. Children composing need the opportunity to:

- explore resources such as voices, instruments and sounds from the environment (General Programme of Study KS1)
- explore and use a widening range of sound sources (KS2)

However, as mentioned earlier, the approach to 'exploring sound' can vary. Does the child have a space where the sounds made can be easily heard? Is the provision of sound sources varied and stimulating within itself? Are there starting points which readily 'get the child going', and then encourage focused attention on investigation and observation of detail? Are the starting points in any way building on previously shared musical experiences – perhaps a song sung together in class or a rhyme chanted together?

The processes that the pupils are engaged in are, indeed, very similar to those used when creating a poem, story, play or even a report. From the range of (sound) sources available, the young composer/creator will begin to **select** and **sequence** the (musical) material. This will involve them **listening** and **deciding** or **judging**, which material best suits their purposes, which captures the essence of what they want to express or represent. Particular musical forms or structures may also be selected, just in the same way a poem may take on the form of a Haiku or acrostic poem. For example, the composition may include questions being asked on instruments with a dynamically contrasting answer given with voices. Here, the initial process of planning may be involved; the young composer(s) designing an outline, structure or framework, which then determines the rationale for their selection of sound sources and other dynamic effects as the music emerges. The National Curriculum documents support this, stating that 'Pupils should be **taught** to:

- explore, create, select and organise sounds in simple structures (e.g. with a beginning, a middle and an end, KS1)
- use sounds and structures to achieve an intended effect (e.g. to create a particular mood, KS2)
- record their compositions using symbols where appropriate and communicate simple musical ideas to others, KS1)

And just as with collaborative writing, group compositions can be a way of ensuring that all pupils, no matter how different their abilities, can participate and share in every stage of the process. This is the springboard for improvising. Defined as 'the act of composing as one goes along' (Hanks, 1979), improvisation involves working creatively with musical ideas, materials and sound patterns in numerous combinations, arising from the interaction and exchange with other performers. The greater the repertoire of musical ideas, sound patterns and sources, the more varied will be the improvised options. It can also encourage a pupil to respond immediately to what has been happening musically. Have they been able to perceive the former sounds as loud and, therefore, possibly followed with loud then quieter sounds? If such contrasts had not been either part of their own play and explorations, or facilitated by the teacher on previous musical encounters, it is likely that this kind of improvised response would not have been part of that child's stored musical understanding.

'The three processes of 'play', 'exploration' and 'improvisation' are fundamental to composing in that each, in a particular and practical way, draws creatively on musical resources within and allows for these to emerge in such a way as to feed into the compositional process. They allow room for trying out and assimilating musical ideas which have been observed and borrowed, as well as those which arise newly from the players, instruments or materials themselves.'
(Glover and Ward (eds), 1993)

The National Curriculum Document (SCAA 1994) states pupils should:

- improvise musical patterns (KS1)
- improve rhythmic and melodic ideas, and arrange music (e.g. add percussion to a song, KS2)

While compositions can sometimes be relatively 'private', improvisations are usually part of a performance situation and involve participating with others.

CHILDREN AS PERFORMERS – INTERPRETERS, DIRECTORS AND ARRANGERS

It is often said that all children 'love to perform'. Implicit in this kind of performing is a 'showing-off'; a bid to be the centre of attention. However, in a musical situation, this is not always true or desirable. Not all children jump at the opportunity to sing solo or to demonstrate a musical pattern in front of the rest of the class. Just as many adults shy clear of such music performance situations, it is not surprising that some pupils also retreat in the face of an audience. Neither would it be appropriate to suggest that a musical performance situation was always the context for show-off behaviour. Clearly, then, being a 'performer' in a musical situation needs to be clarified.

Music is an art form that is realised by performance – the performer's unique role being that of mediator between the composition itself and the audience. Context becomes important. Is the audience present or will they receive the performance by listening to the radio or watching television or a video? Whether the audience is listening to a recording of the composition or to a live performance of it, the soloist or group of musicians will have been busy responding to the instructions given by the composer. But, whether ideas about the performance are given verbally or through notation, the performers actually do much more than merely replicating the exact instructions given. Their **interpretation** of the instructions can be crucial. The context will influence this. Sometimes instructions such as 'press the tape recorder' cannot be altered. It may also be essential for the style of music. Imagine slavishly following the markings from a composer's score; getting faster, louder, quieter, playing smoothly (legato), etc., as indicated.

While the technical side of the performance may not be faulted, we as listeners may have found the performance very sterile and lacking feeling. What needs to happen is that, as the performers get to know and rehearse the work, there is an interaction with the actual notes and the way they are or can be played; the music is being 'brought to life', either via the voice or instrument, or a combination of the two.

Interpretation suggests that the player is making decisions and choices from a range of possible techniques and procedures and knowledge of the possible conventions to which the music may adhere. Children ought to be encouraged to make these musical decisions. They should be encouraged to try performing the piece in several different ways, listening carefully and then being able to discuss before settling for one approach.

> 'If children are to become "musicians" they will be required to learn something of the "workings" of music through action. This involves assimilating and coming to understand the basic *procedural* principles of the discipline.'
> (Plummeridge, 1991, p. 49)

The processes include a continual investigation and development of skills and understanding about how sounds can be manipulated and controlled. This may also include a consideration of the style or genre of the music. If we want to compose some music to accompany our drama project on the Tudors and Stuarts, how can the music we 'compose' actually help to create a feeling of that time? First, we must listen to music from that period (1485–1603). Coming to understand about the musical conventions used at that time; hearing the timbre of the instruments used in those days and having some appreciation of how the various musical materials were combined, will help the young composer/performer recreate the 'music' of the day.

Track 67 ▭

Track 67 is an example of what a group of KS2 pupils composed after hearing some Tudor music.

Maybe the music to be performed adheres to a particular structural procedure which involves several players and would normally be directed or conducted. Imagine a musical sequence where there were opportunities for each player to improvise separately. The conductor would select the order of players and be responsible for bringing every other player in together when required.

Tracks 68 and 69 ▭

Tracks 68 and 69 contain a jazz sequence followed by two pupils' versions. First, you will hear a girl who, upon hearing the music tried to incorporate something she heard into her composition. Clearly she was taken with the 'jumps' which she

heard the saxophone player making. Secondly, a child can be heard trying to pick out the rhythmic pattern heard from the original track, playing a xylophone.

Sometimes, the information available from the composer is insufficient or requires modification for the given group of performers. Perhaps the vocal range cannot be met by the singers, or the skills of the players are limited. In this instance, the performers may modify or **arrange** the music to suit the combination of players. This is another form of interpretation.

Tracks 70 and 71 ▭

Tracks 70 and 71 first give an African drumming sequence (performed by AKLOWA (Cobbson, 1982)), followed by a class arrangement on the most appropriate instruments available (including cardboard boxes!).

In this way, performing and composing are quite closely linked. Many musical processes are common to both, not least that of listening. The composer may be working with sounds heard internally, and be seeking to reproduce these with the instruments and/or voices available. On the other hand, the young composer may be 'inventing' as they investigate sound possibilities, and be making judgements on the immediate external sounds they hear.

CHILDREN BEHAVING MUSICALLY

Many spontaneous activities which children engage in around a music table, in the playground, around the piano, or to accompany a guitar being played, are situations in which children could be observed behaving musically. This may at first seem quite daunting, especially if 'musical' immediately conjures up negative thoughts about being able to 'play instruments'. Actually, such technical skills are not what is

necessarily being referred to. Consider the following list of processes:

anticipate	memorise
identify	play/design
select and sequence	repeat
extending	arrange

In another situation, say technology or design, or even a language activity, we could be looking

Figure 67   Children working together on composition

for pupils who were doing some or maybe all of the above. And are we experts in these fields? Yet somehow we know the significance of these processes in relation to the form, and therefore value any evidence we notice of their existence. Most of us will not be trained designers or linguists, and yet we have learnt for ourselves, or at least understood, that these processes are crucial in the journey towards our pupils becoming more skilled in these areas. Indeed, our observations may lead us to believe that our pupils were on the road to 'behaving like . . . a designer or a linguist or a musician'. It is perhaps ironic then that we are often hesitant to consider how these processes might appear as part of a 'musical' journey.

Coming to understand our pupils' possible musical behaviour is crucial if we are to monitor progress or, indeed, be able to offer assistance with extension and development.

Sometimes pupils will surprise you. The child whom you have been led to believe is a slow learner, may, given the opportunity, demonstrate abilities in a musical context you would not have expected. While seemingly struggling with sequence in language, a child may be able to sequence musical patterns from memory by correctly ordering certain players in the group to repeat the playing of their musical contribution. Another child may be off-task in many other subject areas, but respond well to the particular structure adopted in another teacher's music time.

Another pupil, considered a 'problem in other situations', may well be a blessing in disguise in a music situation, because of their natural talent on a drum or other instrument, or by the way in which they can pick up tunes on the keyboard or remember patterns used from the week before.

While we may readily expect this to be the case ('Oh, they are no good at other subjects but they love music'), as teachers involved in providing educational experiences, our knowledge and understanding need to go beyond these kind of glib generalisations. For if we are able to understand the processes in which these children are able to succeed, we may discover 'keys' for opening other areas of understanding. Here, indeed, we would be able to build on what the learner is bringing to the learning situation – their particular motivation and/or particular way of thinking. One child may just be hearing a set pattern of sounds of different lengths, while another may have translated this into a musical phrase that 'feels unfinished' and needs, they suggest, some additional sounds. At this 'feeling' level, the child in question is responding to the overall pattern, or phrase. He or she may also suggest that in the context of the other instruments being used, it might be more appropriately played on a different instrument for a better effect. What can he or she hear that maybe you as the teacher cannot? Why not let him/her try out the suggestion, and offer the class or group the opportunity to hear for themselves the alternative possibility? Which one did they like best and why? After all, it should be about *their* interpretation.

THE BONUS OF CULTURAL DIVERSITY

Some of your pupils may come from cultural backgrounds which differ from your own. This does not mean that they will have a superior knowledge of the music from that culture. Remember, not all homes are 'musical homes'. While there may be prior musical experiences on which to draw, a key consideration should be that the kind of sounds heard may have been different in timbre, rhythmic patterning and pitch sequences, and, indeed, the way the elements were combined in different contexts. How we organise sounds to signify the sentiments of a funeral may be completely different in another culture, where death is considered not an ending, but a beginning. While we may combine long, smooth sounds with a slow pulse, another culture may organise the combinations in such a way to suggest to our ears a party, with a more lively tempo, energetic rhythms, and a bright-sounding melody line. But, of course, that is what a funeral in that culture is about – a more joyous occasion.

The pupil's previous experiences may include dancing, singing, playing different instruments or some combination of these. While the child may not initially have the language with which to communicate these experiences, providing situations where these strengths can be demonstrated is essential. But why should a 'good dancer' be adept, at age six, to dance to what might seem completely foreign-sounding music?

As adults, we may be good at rock'n'roll, but hesitate at dancing the salsa from Latin America. Therefore, it is important that we enable all pupils to demonstrate their musical understandings at their own levels in their own ways. If this means the use of visual clues (see Chapter 2) or the inclusion of music 'new to us' in our movement periods or the searching for soundtracks from the cultural backgrounds present in our classes, so be it – after all, they are required by law to be at school, whereas we are choosing to be there!

In this way, too, it is possible to ask pupils to recognise and distinguish similarities and differences in the music heard. What musical aspects are the same or different? Are the feelings evoked the same or different?

Possibly you and your pupils all share the same cultural background, and you may feel that this section is of little significance to you. The National Curriculum gives some guidance on this point. Introductory statements KS1/2:

'The repertoire chosen for performing and listening should extend pupils' musical experience and knowledge, and develop appreciation of the richness of our diverse cultural heritage. It should include music in a variety of styles from different times and places.' (SCAA, 1994)

Therefore, it is important that we embrace a range of world music so that our pupils experience a rich musical education.

Remember:

- **Your learners may not always be able to hear** – many children at some time in their lives suffer from hearing loss (due to catarrh, glue ear or other ailments). So when a child does not participate in a musical activity in the way you expect, consider the possibility that even a temporary hearing impairment may be affecting their perception and ability to listen, not only to your instructions, but also to the sounds involved during the music activity. They may not be able to perceive as easily certain kinds of sounds, making enthusiastic wild guesses, rather than not participating. This can often be misleading for us as teachers.

- **Your learners may not all be well coordinated** – poor eye and hand coordination may affect how well a pupil can sustain the fluent reading and playing of music. Others may have difficulty hearing and/or feeling the pulse, which will affect their ability to articulate the required steady pattern. Not all pupils may be able to use both hands when playing instruments, tapping out body sounds, etc., and may need more practice at this skill. Those having difficulty should not be excluded, but given greater opportunities to improve their skills.

- **Your learners need to receive equal access to music activities** and the range of classroom instruments available. We often find more boys than girls playing drums and dominating available electronic equipment, unless we as teachers work to actively encourage space for the girls to be involved. More girls than boys seem to participate in choirs. This can be counteracted in numerous ways, such as by encouraging male staff to participate to provide suitable role models; and by carefully considering the repertoire. Try to avoid 'mushy' lyrics, which boys may feel uncomfortable with at first. Sentiments are usually also reflected in the music, which should be kept bright and energetic. Once the children are enjoying choir work with you, then a wider range of styles can be introduced.

There is now an increasing number of book and music collections which clearly acknowledge the contribution that women have made to the field of music. An active and conscious effort to ensure that music by women composers/performers is included in the listening repertoire should be made. This could be reinforced by working towards there being a balance of female and male performers in any live performances introduced to the school.

- **Your learners may include some pupils who are musically gifted** – some may already be receiving private lessons, but others may not. These pupils need to be extended and encouraged, and opportunities for this should be found within lessons and the musical provisions in the school. Can their instruments be included in the group compositions? This is surely an extension for them – such pupils would be involved in improvising and composing, which may not be part of their particular instrumental tuition anyway.

- **Your learners may have feelings which have not previously been expressed** – for some children, the expression of feelings and emotions is a particularly painful area. Possibly the forms of expression are considered inappropriate by others, or the feelings are withheld, the young child not knowing how to give voice to them. There is little disagreement that music has many powers to affect our emotions. Beyond mere catharsis, music education provides opportunities to understand and explore our feelings. Previously, I have talked about the inner and the external world of sound and of play. Music deals with the memories of feelings and imagined feelings, rather than feelings by themselves. Music can deal with feelings removed from specific events, thereby providing space in which to build artistic structures that teach and enthral. Perhaps that is why every culture and civilisation has found in music a means for identifying and understanding its most elusive and profound feelings.

LEARNING IN MUSIC

With the weighting 2:1 in favour of Attainment Target 1 'Composing and performing', there can be little doubt that the emphasis should be on 'doing' music. However, nowhere is there a suggestion that 'products' should be more important than the 'process'; indeed, the two are interlocked, which makes the artificial separation into AT1 and AT2 appear most distressing and unmusical.

Certain kinds of learning are essential for musical doing. Being able to 'imagine' music (a process) will certainly assist with the process of producing a composition (product). Similarly, it could be said that we need to learn to 'anticipate' music if we are going to learn how to perform or conduct it. Part of this anticipation may also be the imagining or the internal hearing of the music. Could some processes be prerequisites for others? Certainly the interaction between musical sounds and ourselves appears to be at the heart of the musical experience. Planning for this musical experience involves a consistent awareness of how people and sounds are interacting. The interaction becomes the experience, and the experience is the heart of the educational process.

COLLABORATIVE LEARNING

One's response to, and relationship with, music is an individual phenomena. However, due to space and time, the making of music (composing) in schools is most frequently a collaborative venture. Each learner brings to the situation their own perceptions, feelings and imaginings – their own experiences and repertoire of musical sounds, sensations and memories. It is in collaborative group work that pupils can pool these, experiment with the possibilities and then make considered judgements or decisions about what they will use and why, having arrived at some form of shared meaning.

A quick glance back at the list under the heading 'Remember your learners . . .' (see p. 61) will remind you that among a class of pupils there will be a whole range of needs and capabilities. Planned musical encounters will ensure that all of these pupils can be catered for.

However, group work may not always be collaborative. While the former may ensure 'products' at the end of a specified time, the participants in the group may have experienced very different learning processes. Stereotyped characters come to mind – the bully, the know-all, the dreamer, the uncoordinated, the social clown, the musically gifted, etc. For each, the 'group experience' may be more memorable than the focused selection and organisation of sounds.

Chapter 4 addresses the role of the teacher, suggesting ways in which musical activities can be organised within the use of a 'framework' to enhance the learning of music.

SUGGESTIONS

1 Ask the parents of your pupils if they could let you have a copy of some music they play at home, and which the children would listen to in the home environment. (Do not be surprised if some parents say they do not play music at home.) This will help you build up a collection of sound sources.

2 Make a list of the children who seem to enjoy music. Beside their names, write down what has led you to this conclusion. (Some starters: was it a big smile, a spontaneous tapping of the feet, the frequent singing heard or the pleasure at playing instruments?)

3 Set up a 'music corner' using only one kind of sound source, for example, things to shake. Ask the children if they can sort the sounds they make into groups with an explanation for their selection.

4 Reflect on the kind of musical opportunities you presently provide for your pupils. In what ways do they allow pupils to demonstrate a range of musical behaviours?

5 Discuss whether 'play' should be accepted as a process, not necessarily with any outcome. In what ways could musical play be encouraged and valued in your classroom?

6 'Good learners take their time, don't mind asking questions, aren't afraid of saying "I don't know" or of being wrong, can change their minds and enjoy finding out.'
(Claxton, 1984, p. 219)

What are the implications of this statement for teachers with busy classrooms to manage?

The teacher and pedagogy

What do we need to know about teaching music? This is an enormous question, which begs many secondary ones. For instance, how does teaching music differ from teaching other subjects? Or, to put it another way, what similarities are there between teaching music and other subjects? Let us remember all those professional skills and attributes we bring to our work with young learners. Whether it is mathematics, science, history or geography, the same tools of the profession are used – so why not also use them in the teaching of music?

The challenge referred to in Chapter 1 was about how to bring learners and music together in a meaningful context. I would therefore like to begin this chapter with a reminder of some of those things we already do as teachers, using some time-honoured headings to help us.

THE TOOLS FOR TEACHING

There are numerous studies which draw attention to the way a teacher's approach can affect both the learner and the type of learning achieved. One of the key factors determining 'teacher style' is personal motivation. If we are 'doing music' merely because it is a National Curriculum requirement, clearly our personal engagement with the subject will be minimal. If, on the other hand, we want to 'do music' with our pupils because we actually think that music is important, that it can be fun, and that musical activities are important for young learners to experience, our commitment will be clearly different.

With this latter view, the teacher will be concerned with both 'processes' and 'products'. The model of an 'empty vessel being filled up with wonderful music, knowledge and skills' is replaced with that of active participation in musical processes, behaviours and situations. Our focus, therefore, is on the pupil learning, not our own weaknesses. The General Programme of Study states: 'In all Key Stages pupils should be given opportunities to . . .', and under the Key Stage-specific Programmes of Study, 'pupils should be taught to . . .'. The onus then is on the teacher. But what does this really mean? Why is it that we will allow groups of children to work on maths, while others work on a language activity, while still others work on a history task, and yet in music we tend to think of all pupils 'doing' music together at the same time? Was that the model we had of how to teach music from our own schooling? Perhaps initial teacher training has indeed changed over the years. At least this should reassure us! After all, what we should feel confident about is a knowledge of how pupils learn, about educational psychology, even if we are not science, history or music graduates!

Here is a list of some of these professional skills.

- classroom management – seating, routines, grouping, organisation of lessons

- selecting appropriate materials to match the abilities/interests in a class
- identifying areas of learning difficulty/expertise
- types of questions and their advantages and/or consequences
- diagnosing problem areas (skills, cognition, motivation) (see Chapter 5)
- identifying changes and monitoring pupils' development (see Chapter 5)
- the sequencing of activities in such a way as to assist the learner to acquire new understandings, revisit and build on previous knowledge, and to reinforce and apply understanding to new situations
- being able to decode or break down an activity which involves certain skills, or a number of different pieces of information, into its constituent parts and to order these

- being able to facilitate situations where the pupils can make their own discoveries and can investigate, select and organise and try out
- knowing the strategies for and being able to give clear explanations
- being able to respond appropriately to a range of pupil utterances and behaviours in ways that both encourage, extend and help the young learner to develop (see Chapter 5)
- being able to develop positive and supportive relationships with pupils, knowing what and where the boundaries are.

This list could go on. As indicated, some areas will be dealt with in Chapter 5, but I shall consider a few general headings in more detail.

TEACHING STYLES

The style or approach you adopt will affect how you choose to organise both the children and the resources within your room. Research into classrooms (Elliott, 1976; Galton, Simon and Croll, 1980; Gipps, 1992; Struthers, 1991–2; Wragg and Bennett, 1988–91) suggests that teachers may use a range of styles in any one day, and while dealing with any one area of the curriculum. As each 'style' does appear to have a consequence for the learners, what are the effects of different styles of teaching in a music context? I shall use four pairs of terms, no doubt easily recognisable, that arose from the work in the Ford Teaching Project (Elliott, 1976).

Formal or informal?

For many, these terms may conjure up scenes of tightly controlled, synchronised chime-bar tapping on the one hand and, on the other hand,

total chaos with children, instruments and sounds all over the place! Whatever imagery these two terms suggest to you, they are the result of how a teacher has decided to organise the learning situation. Such extremes should never be encouraged. However, imagine the beginning of a lesson where, after revisiting the concepts used in a previous week, the teacher wishes to introduce the concept for this session. It may also be considered necessary to remind the learners of the rules around the handling of instruments. As all pupils need to be part of this 'introduction', it will be necessary for the teacher to establish a more formal ambience; one which involves the teacher talking and the pupils listening.

This may then change into a different mode; opportunities are given for the learners to gradually become more active and independent in their efforts to grapple with the content of the subject.

Dependent or independent?

A traditional image may involve the teacher beside the piano, with all the pupils on the floor in front of him or her, following musical direction, being totally reliant on the teacher as the source of knowledge. At the other extreme, the teacher's style would involve a detachment from the learners, who would be expected to be active and totally independent in their search for knowledge. The intermediate stance would allow for both modes to be present (my own bias is to encourage a swing towards the independent problem-solving capabilities of the learner). They would be encouraged to investigate, select and organise the sound sources in the way they chose, free from explicit teacher direction. Of course, there are times when it is appropriate to offer learners well-structured and planned encounters with musical ideas, concepts and even repertoire. And it may be worthwhile to initially create the space for the learner to 'try out' the use of a skill, musical material or a combination of expressive musical forms in a structured context.

For example: the class are looking at 'dynamics' and have worked in numerous ways with loud and quiet. A **structured context** may involve the whole class in echo-copying the loud or quiet tambourine sounds from a tape, first by clapping and then with instruments. (This could equally be organised as a small group activity around a 'listening post'.) A more **inventive context** may extend this activity. In a circle, the first child plays a known or improvised rhythm with a particular dynamic. The next child at first imitates the previously heard pattern and dynamics before adding his or her own invented dynamic pattern (which may be similar or different).

Structured or unstructured?

As with the above descriptions, this kind of teacher approach refers to the ability of the teacher to allow (or not) the pupils to have some control over, and definition of, their own learning. It is often dependent on the teacher's personal need to feel secure and in control. Little wonder, then, that we may have memories of music teachers who ran very structured and controlled lessons – either they knew a lot about music and very little about actual pedagogical styles or how children learnt, or their tight rein on the situation was due to their anxiety about the subject area itself! Hopefully, you won't find yourself in that situation.

Guided or open-ended?

Can you imagine yourself asking questions that encourage the learners to investigate, challenge former understandings and contemplate possibilities, all in music? To do this, you yourself need to be an 'inquirer'. The questions you may ask will be those of your own musical journey, and they will demonstrate to the learner a model of an adult who is inquisitive and eager to try new things – someone who does not know it all!

Perhaps the key words in the above are 'journey' and 'know it all'. Musical understanding, as discussed in previous chapters, is evolutionary; it is based on the impact of musical encounters and the acquisition of knowledge and skills and, as such, can never be something fixed. The nature of music and the expressive qualities radiating from the sounds in combination, mean that these sounds can both represent our inner worlds and, at the same time, be analogous to feelings and states actually being experienced. In this way, we are all interpreters, and there can never be any one right answer; we can never really say we know it all. Indeed, there would never be so many different recordings available of certain works if that were the case.

Picture another scenario, where the teacher is providing very little guidance as to what the learners may discover, what they could do next or what might be a possible aspect to develop further. This extreme suggests a very limited understanding of both learners, the subject matter and/or effective styles of teaching.

CLASSROOM MANAGEMENT

Without a doubt, all the styles described above involve different ways of managing the learning setting – from the routines established and the organisation of chairs, to the size of the group, and the choice of materials for the lesson. Depending on what it is hoped the learners will achieve, the teacher may choose to begin his or her lesson with the whole class. Will this be with the class on the floor near you, or will they stay at their desks for the introduction? Your decisions about managing resources and learners may be influenced by numerous factors:

• the age of the learners
• their previous musical experiences and routines (are they familiar with collaborative group work, handling instruments, working independently, musical procedures, etc.?)
• the chemistry of the class (the characters within it)
• the space available – classroom, music room or hall (if in the hall, you may have the pupils seated on individual chairs or benches in a semicircle)
• the type of activity planned (group activities with instruments, listening, class singing with some pupils playing instrumental accompaniments, movement, recording or 'fixing' compositions)
• the location of the instruments (are they stored in movable 'family' trays or boxes (all claves and wood blocks, all triangles with beaters, all shakers, all tambourines)? Are there enough pairs of beaters? Instruments may be on a trolley which needs to be collected by a pupil from another class in the first few minutes of the lesson, or they may need to be removed from cupboards, etc.)

• whether you wish all pupils to move at the same pace (that is, all have a go before moving on to something else) or whether you aim to differentiate by task or by outcome
• whether you will be observing or monitoring any of the pupils' work during the lesson, and will, therefore, require a particular organisational framework or structure
• whether you have pupils with visual or hearing impairments who need to be considered in terms of where they sit or who they work with
• whether you have pupils who may be able to offer assistance because of their personal music backgrounds

The list could continue, but what will have become evident is that many of the concerns here are no different to those tabled for consideration in other subject areas. Thus the teaching of music needs to be seen not as some uniquely different task, but instead as a task that you are qualified to participate in.

VERBAL BEHAVIOUR

The National Curriculum refers to 'appraising' music in conjunction with listening and/or making music. The term refers to 'talking about music', and talk is a very significant component in the process of education. Naturally, the way we talk and the vocabulary that we use is also very important to this process (Barnes, 1981). We are able to convey meaning, value and/or bias both about the subject area and the learner.

Let us consider three different vocabularies that can be employed to assist the educative process in music. Tait and Haack (1984) call these the professional, experiential and behavioural vocabularies.

The primary function of the **professional** vocabulary is to describe the sound phenomena as accurately as possible. There are words to describe the physical properties, such as vibration, intonation, duration, attack, release, timbre. And there are still other words which describe the formal properties of music, which have been referred to as 'musical elements' in the National Curriculum, and as 'materials' elsewhere in the text: rhythm, dynamics, structure, pitch, etc. Finally, we also talk about music's aesthetic properties, which involves vocabulary such as shape, colour, balance, pattern, line and style.

The **experiential** vocabulary 'balances what is heard and perceived with what is felt' (Barnes, 1981, p. 78). It is significant because it helps to bridge the gap between music and the learners. It describes the individual response to sounds and brings together what is heard with what is felt, what is imagined and what is sensed, what is analysed and what is reflected upon. The vocabulary may be in terms of an image, such as an event, a place or a colour. It may take the form of a metaphor dealing with a quality of feeling or movement, such as eager, calm, energetic or surprised, or it may refer to life processes and include such words as growth, decay, cohesion or tension.

The final vocabulary is **behavioural** and refers to all the behaviours learners can demonstrate when they interact with music. Some behaviours will be more about considered, rational thought responses, such as analysing, defining, identifying and comparing. Others will be at a level of basic feeling, such as sensing, exploring, imagining and elaborating. Some will be more social and stress

communicative processes, such as performing, describing, explaining, rehearsing and asking.

These categories are not fixed. Many word meanings can flow from one category to another. Indeed, as with music itself, there are most often ambiguities. Poetry speaks to each listener or reader in different ways, a word may draw upon different feelings within, conjure up different memories, different imagery. We would most often be drawing on a combination of vocabularies. Our understanding of the language we use in conjunction with the type of questions we ask is an important tool of teaching.

Here are some examples of statements and questions you might use in your classroom.

Professional vocabulary:
- Clap a rhythmic phrase from this verse.
- Can you identify what the structure of this piece is?
- In what way was the second verse a variation on the first verse?
- What made Mhyra's group performance feel so together?

Experiential vocabulary:
- Can you make this music flow?
- This is a piece of music that is full of energy.
- Oh, you just whizzed through that like a rocket!
- Did the piece feel finished to you, ending like that?

Behavioural vocabulary:
- Can you say in what way those two patterns were similar?
- How many different sounds could you hear on the tape?
- Imagine you are creeping through the jungle. Which extract best describes how you would be moving?
- Explore this instrument and see how many different sounds you can make.
- Clap this pattern for the whole group.
- Can you demonstrate the shape of this melody in the air?

QUESTIONS

The kinds of questions the teacher asks will reveal to the pupil the kind of thinking which is expected of them. Questions may be quite simple, involving memory recall, for example, 'How many did we count to come in before?' This type are usually referred to as closed questions; they are so worded to suggest that there is just one correct answer. Questions which leave space for the answer to take numerous forms are ones which demand higher levels of thinking. Bloom (1956) has identified six levels of questions. The questions at each level require a response which uses a different kind of thought process. They appear below, along with key words or phrases matched with each level:

LEVELS	KEY WORDS OR PHRASES
1 Knowledge/ LOWER recall	who? what? when? where? define, recognise, recall, identify
2 Comprehension	describe, compare, contrast, explain, rephrase
3 Application	apply, solve, classify, select, use, give an example
4 Analysis HIGHER	why? what factors? draw conclusions, deduce, identify, cause and reason, discriminate
5 Synthesis	predict, propose, plan, write, develop, what would happen if ...
6 Evaluation	judge, evaluate, decide, appraise, give own opinion, justify

Figure 68 Bloom's six levels of questions

What becomes significant about this list is that it enables us to focus on the nature of the activities the pupils will be engaged in – a vital component for monitoring pupil progress (see Chapter 5).

Using these levels, you can plan a differentiated programme, where the pupils are able to work at their own levels, in and across a number of musical contexts – singing, playing, creating, directing, moving, reading/writing and discussing.

Research on questioning is thought-provoking (Galton, Simon and Croll, 1980). While evidence seems to suggest that there is a dominance of recall and managerial type questions being asked, Dillon (1981) argues that excessive questioning can evoke anxiety and dependence. In their work from the Leverhulme Primary Project, Brown and Wragg (1993) suggest that 'the only conclusion that can be drawn from this is that you have to choose what kinds of learning you want to promote and then choose appropriate types of questions'. Since evidence confirms that children are capable of generating more exploratory questions, hypotheses and explanations when teachers were not present, it leaves little doubt that collaborative group work in music may be a more appropriate management strategy for some types of musical learning experiences. Whatever strategy we adopt, it is not only the questions we ask, but also how and why we ask them that need to be considered. How are we sounding when we pose the question? The quality of articulation can dramatically affect the impact of the message. Pupils are on the look-out for hidden meanings and will be very quick to detect your sarcasm, your insecurity, your boredom, etc. Your voice can be a very powerful tool in more ways than just the musical situation!

Of course, the learning context is very important when considering vocabulary. Teachers should be sensitive to different ethnic minority groups who are likely to have unique vocabularies, dialects or methods of articulation. Incorporating some words from their vocabularies into the music situation is suggested. Care and consideration should also be taken to consider the language needs of those learners with specific learning needs and impairments. Do we exclude those pupils who have English as a second language (ESL) from our lessons because of our use of adjectives which they are not familiar with? Could visual representations be found which invite consensus and then the English word equivalent?

Brown and Wragg (1993) remind us of the power of language, confirming that the vocabularies we use for each subject are as significant as the questions we ask in our efforts to provide 'learning' experiences for our pupils:

> 'It seems to us that these findings show how important discussion and free play of language are for developing understanding. One strategy to use in this respect is to explore the patterns of thinking of pupils in their own terms and then to show links with the language and assumptions of a subject'.
> (Brown and Wragg, 1993, p.11)

NON-VERBAL BEHAVIOUR

Music is a non-verbal art. Therefore, it is obvious that the ways of knowing and understanding music could potentially involve significant components of non-verbal communication.

The most obvious non-verbal behaviour with the body or a part of the body is that apparent when 'conducting or directing'. Even when we use our hands to trace the shape of a melodic phrase, for example the step-downward movements for 'Three blind mice', we are giving a visual model. Our gestures can communicate dynamic growth or decline, a range of intense or sudden changes, and even specific technical skills, such as how to tap the chime bar or change the sounds made on the 'cabasa Afuche'.

Non-verbal behaviour can also be used to communicate expressive qualities. The body can be used to illustrate a quality of feeling or some characteristic movement which the sounds can be interpreted to represent.

The point that needs to be stressed is that, just as verbal behaviour is a two-way connection with questions and statements, so too is non-verbal behaviour. The learner and the teacher should be involved together in this form of communication.

Figure 69   Playing cabasa afuche

The anticipation of when to 'come in' can be felt and signalled with the body (hands, shoulders, eyes) as can the release of tension when the piece begins.

Figure 70 A group performance

APPROACHING THE PLANNING OF A MUSIC PROGRAMME

It is thought in some circles that, with a Music National Curriculum document 'on the table', teachers should have no problems or dilemmas planning and providing music for young learners. However, separating musical experience into Attainment Targets and Programmes of Study has not proved to be a constructive way to approach the provision of musical experiences, knowledge and skills.

However, the Draft Proposals have brought the elements into a more prominent position, with the Attainment Targets also being presented in a less separate way. I shall begin to consider ways in which a spiral framework (with musical elements) can help us to think about developing musical understanding. Naturally, the sequencing of activities may seem a logical way forward. But

what musical understanding could be drawn from each activity? Do these also have some sequential development? What skills are involved in each activity? Is there a progressive sequence to the skill development inherent in each? It seems that an activity-driven approach may run into the danger of being like a collection of 'bright ideas'.

Field-tested over many years, this spiral framework offers less risk of such an *ad hoc* approach. At the heart of the spiral (as originally conceived by Jerome Bruner, 1960) is the belief that the musical materials can be understood and utilised in ever increasing degrees of sophistication. The nursery child may already have a repertoire of sounds and musical shapes within his or her grasp, acquired even before arriving at the nursery. As 'raw' materials, these will continue to be used, but with classification and language attributed to them, these same sounds and shapes begin to take on new meanings. It is as if the young child can actually 'do more with' his or her original collection, because it has become slightly more refined. Certainly, as understanding grows, there seem to be more opportunities available; greater choice exists. No longer can he or she get just one sound from the tambourine, but several sounds are possible. This development may have involved increased motor coordination (he/she can now play in different ways – speed, dynamics, sounds produced), coupled with a growing range of adjectives to describe the sounds and maybe a growing set of labels (adverbs) for the way the sounds have actually been made (shaking, tapping, stroking, etc.). Also, the child will have had the opportunity to 'play' the instrument with others, and will have added to this bank of sound, both in terms of sound qualities and sound quantities.

It is hardly surprising, then, that the spiral itself visually shows this evolving complexity.

Pre-Key Stage 1 learners can be engaged at every turn of the spiral, and they will then be able to re-visit their understanding regularly in subsequent years. One hopes that the musical

experiences through a child's schooling will provide opportunities for growth in the understanding of the musical materials. Experience of the elements, both separately and in numerous different combinations with others, should be part of the child's educational growth.

It is the growing understanding of the musical materials that actually affects the quality of the musical sounds produced in the subsequent range of activities provided. If young learners have not had the opportunity to investigate the kind of sounds possible on voice and instrument, how can they, on a later occasion, have an extended repertoire from which to select sounds for their compositions? If they have not had the opportunity to tap both knees simultaneously, gradually doing different things with each hand (beat with the left hand and tapping rhythm with the right hand), how can we hope that they will be ready to manipulate two or more beaters on a tuned instrument or coordinate two hands on a keyboard or other instrument?

This may seem a mere coordination skill. However, for the child to then have a bank of ideas about how sounds can be changed or organised in a sequence, he or she needs to have encountered those materials/elements/concepts at some point.

Figure 71   Using both hands to demonstrate pulse

Figure 72   Playing class instruments with both hands

Figure 73   Playing keyboards with two hands

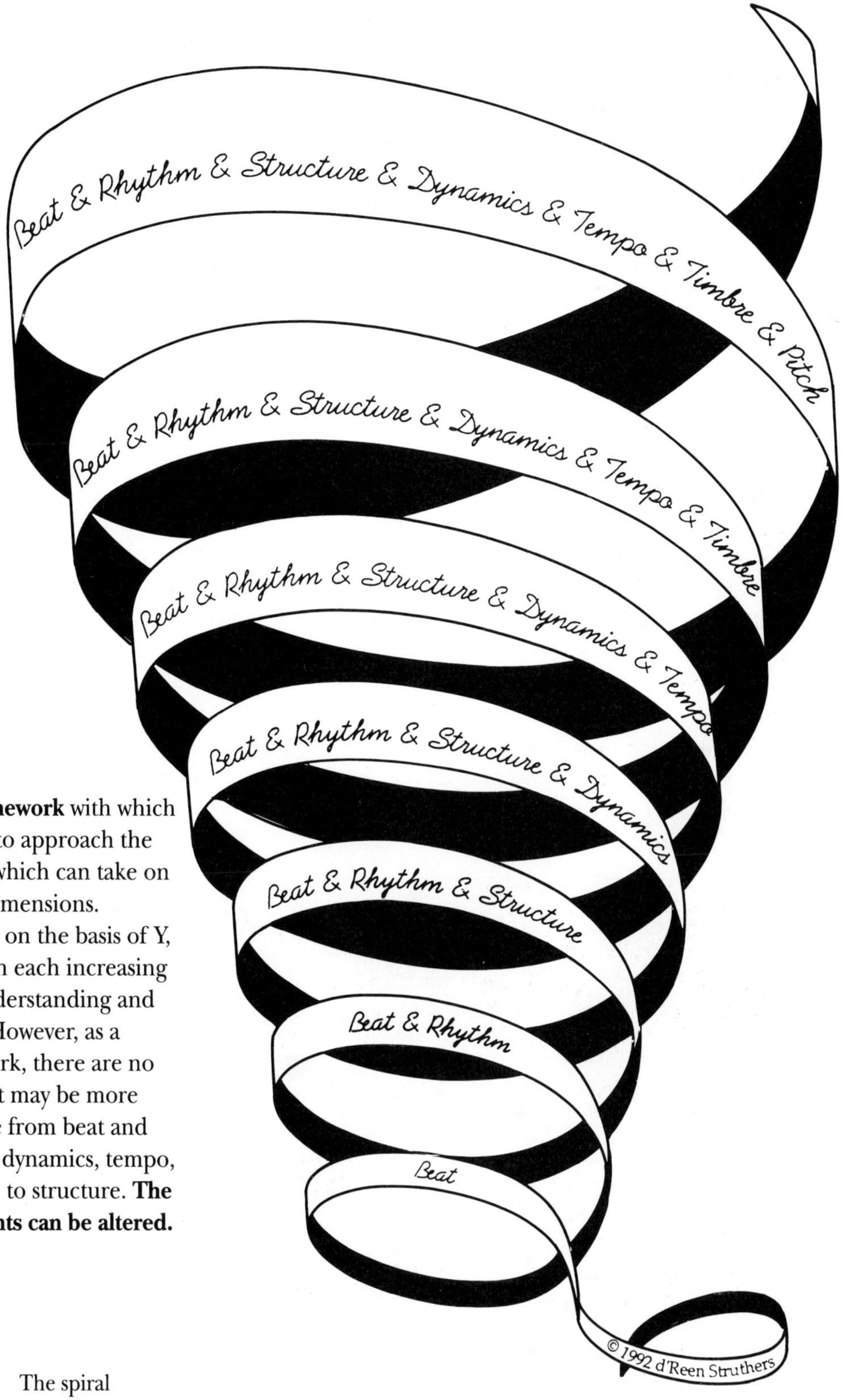

The spiral offers a **framework** with which a teacher can begin to approach the provision of activities which can take on truly musical dimensions.

The spiral functions on the basis of Y, Y+1, Y+1+2, etc., with each increasing layer adding new understanding and musical insight. However, as a scaffolding/framework, there are no fixed procedures. It may be more appropriate to move from beat and rhythm to questions of dynamics, tempo, pitch, timbre and then to structure. **The order of the components can be altered.**

In the spiral (reading from bottom to top):

Beat

Beat & Rhythm

Beat & Rhythm & Structure

Beat & Rhythm & Structure & Dynamics

Beat & Rhythm & Structure & Dynamics & Tempo

Beat & Rhythm & Structure & Dynamics & Tempo & Timbre

Beat & Rhythm & Structure & Dynamics & Tempo & Timbre & Pitch

© 1992 d'Reen Struthers

Figure 74   The spiral

The draft document states that 'Although the Programmes of Study have been set out in relation to each Attainment Target, there is no implication that teaching activities or learning opportunities should be designed to address them separately.' Here is a clear indication that there is an awareness that musical experience should not be two separate Attainment Targets.

The General Programme of Study 'defines the opportunities that should be given during each Key Stage. This part is common to all Key Stages, providing continuity of musical experience from five to fourteen'. The six areas described are:

- control sounds
- perform with others
- compose
- refine, record and communicate
- develop knowledge
- respond and evaluate

These six areas then directly relate to the statements in the Key Stage-specific Programme of Study.

However, musical experiences occur in the following contexts:

- singing
- playing
- listening
- moving
- creating
- directing
- reading/writing
- discussing

These contexts are not just to be found in schools, but occur in the wider community. This is very important to note since there has been concern voiced that 'music in schools' is quite unique and not found mirrored or repeated elsewhere in their life experiences. An analysis of the Key Stage-specific Programmes of Study reveals that the contexts described above can indeed be found in the document.

CONTEXTS	KEY STAGE-SPECIFIC PROGRAMME OF STUDY
Singing	a, b, d, e, f, g, i
Playing	c, d, e, f, g, h, i
Listening	see Introductory Statement i, j, k, l, m
Moving	b, c, d, l
Creating	e, f, g, l
Directing	f, g, h, l
Recording/writing	a, b, f, h
Talking about	m

Figure 75 Musical contexts in the National Curriculum

Since the contexts clearly exist within the National Curriculum and beyond as 'constants', we need, then, to consider how the musical materials/elements can be approached in an ever more sophisticated manner. How can each element be revisited across the Key Stages with ever increasing complexity? This is a bit like considering how our understanding and personal experiences of mobility become more complex.

Most babies will first roll, then crawl and then gradually acquire the skill to stand and then walk. The next change will be an interaction with an object (pushing the pushchair, managing the pedal car, the tricycle and then the bicycle). So it is through our lives that we begin to interact with more sophisticated objects as both our understanding and skills improve. The young person may have experienced flying, but they may never actually become a pilot, although simulators now can provide us with this seemingly very real first-hand experience. Of course, even without simulators, we can 'pretend' to be the pilot; our 'play' becoming all the more real, as our understanding of the many things a pilot actually has to deal with grows.

I suggest acquiring musical understanding is similar. Our early musical utterances actually become more advanced as we develop our understanding and skill. Just as many of us do not become pilots or skilled horse-riders, we can at least indulge in imagining what is involved; we can begin to move towards 'behaving like musicians'. With more knowledge, our imagination has more to feed upon, and our 'play' can take on new dimensions. Of course, we may dabble at horse-riding, taking the pony trek along the beach, for example. Now with this first-hand experience our fantasy world reaches new heights. We have the sensations of riding the horse stored now, for use in our story-telling, our dreams and for preparing us for the next trek!

In musical encounters, our senses are able to receive the sounds and, possibly, the physical movements, with the impact of the experience becoming the greater for us. Being able to explain what was happening (maybe using our bodies rather than words, or even pictures) we have now got a starting point from which to 'copy' those feelings. I have observed young children watching a live performance of a string quartet. With both the visual and aural stimulus, they can begin to 'pretend' to be the violinist or the cellist. Even more fascinating is that, when given the opportunity to actually sit with and handle the instruments seen played, they seemed to adopt uncanny likenesses to the players. The players' gestures were copied and, even without the cello-playing skills, the sounds they began to make seemed imbued with the feelings they had clearly observed, and I would suggest felt, in the music they had heard. This renewed my belief that young learners need to have opportunities not only to gradually extend their repertoire of understanding, but also to demonstrate that understanding through their own music-making.

THE FRAMEWORK

Organised in years, each musical element appears, but with ever more sophisticated complexity, alongside the contexts in which these musical materials could be dealt with. Planning and evaluation checklists for years 1–6 can be found in the appendix. Figure 76 shows how 'beat', for example, could be considered in year 1 and in year 4. Clearly, if the groundwork has been covered in earlier years, the need to dwell on beat by year 5 is not necessary for most pupils. By this stage, is has become a 'given' and is the foundation on which more complicated rhythmic patterns can be built. Without a good feeling for, and an understanding of, 'beat/pulse', more

CONTEXTS	KEY STAGE 1 (YEAR 1)	KEY STAGE 2 (YEAR 4)
Singing	Can the children detect the pulse in a song? What happens if the pulse/beat is altered?	Developing their understanding of pulse via the way it may affect the form of the song, the meaning, the way to begin the song together …
Playing	Can the children play instruments keeping the pulse? Are there ways the instruments can be effectively handled/played to sustain a regular pulse? What cues do they need to sustain the pulse/beat?	In their performances, does a greater understanding of pulse affect their group work? Do pupils select a range of pulses to use in their music-making?
Listening	From a range of musics, can the pupils demonstrate the sense of pulse/beat for each?	The pupils' ability to detect different pulse forms should have improved. This can be demonstrated with gesture, imitation of pulse, etc. from music heard.
Moving	Can the children suggest ways to move to different pulses/beats as they hear them changing?	A sense of pulse should be informing their dance patterns, their non-verbal behaviour, and their control of their instruments.
Creating	When the children are involved in making their own music, do they use a sense of pulse/beat?	Where pulse in used, can the pupils demonstrate effective changes of pulse to create different effects for their compositions?
Reading/writing	Can the children discover effective ways to write different pulse/beat patterns? Can their forms of 'notation' be understood by others?	More sophisticated notations can be used, score reading and representations could be investigated in more depth.
Talking about	As a result of their experiences with different pulse patterns, can the pupils talk about how pulse affects the feel of the music for them?	By end of KS2, pupils should have developed a language to talk about the role pulse/beat plays in different music for different occasions, etc.
Directing	Can the pupils 'direct' a musical event, demonstrating their understanding of pulse and the role it plays in music?	A greater dexterity to conduct music with different pulses – observations of conductors – use of different techniques, etc. should be seen.

Figure 76 Music materials – pulse

complicated rhythms cannot be as successfully explored.

Of course, as the pupils become ever more familiar with musical materials, the options for applying their understanding to a widening range of activities becomes extended.

Your planning can then be arranged around this framework, each lesson incorporating elements that have been visited, within the musical contexts. Clearly, this provides a wide variety of experiences for the learner, while also ensuring that their understanding is being reinforced and applied in the range of contexts.

Each lesson should provide opportunities for the pupils to revisit familiar elements and with a variety of different contexts. Forty minutes spent on group singing will not encourage such possibilities. With the 2:1 weighting in favour of the pupils actively engaging in music (AT1 Composing and performing), the following checklist may be helpful.

- Does the lesson include opportunities for the pupils to be involved in a variety of contexts, for example, singing, listening, creating (composing), talking about and reading/writing?
- What musical element(s) will be revisited and what will be new?
- If a new element is to be introduced, how can this be drawn from the existing musical repertoire (for example, a familiar song, a previously recorded composition from the class, a piece of recorded music)?
- How many of the class will be involed in the activity, say, of using instruments?
- Has time been allowed for the pupils to listen to each others' compositions?
- What are the key questions to be asked?
- What new vocabulary will be introduced? In what ways will this be done?
- What are you hoping the lesson will achieve?
- What observations will you be making to monitor whether the learning outcomes have been achieved?
- What specific skills, behaviour or understanding are you hoping to observe?
- What resources will be required (specific types of instruments, charts, cards, tape recorders, recordings, etc.)?
- For what percentage of the lesson will the pupils be actively engaged in either structured or less structured activities?
- Do the activities lend themselves to individual musical utterances, or will they be operating 'in chorus'?

Many of these considerations begin to sound just like the list of things we think about when planning for other subjects. So what are the additional concerns for music? First, music is a very individualised matter. To always insist that children should sing or play in particular ways without providing space for them to demonstrate their own interpretations would be to curb both their enjoyment and their growing understanding.

- Have we provided opportunities for the pupils to express their musical understanding, that is, have they been able to demonstrate their understanding of musical materials by using their bodies, their voices, instruments or combinations of these?
- Have we encouraged them to talk of their feelings about:
  - playing in the group?
  - listening to the piece?
  - the music they have heard?
  - the appropriateness of the symbols used?
  - the effect of how the musical elements have been combined?
  - the conductor's gestures?
  - the effect of using certain instruments?
- Have we encouraged them to talk about their understanding of:
  - the music they have heard?
  - what they thought worked well in the piece and why?
  - what they thought could be improved and why?
  - what they would like to try out?
  - what they imagine a particular change might sound like?
  - what the symbols used might mean?
  - using possibly other symbols for more effective communication?
  - why the conductor moved his or her hands in a certain way?
  - why certain instruments were, or might be, effective?
- Have we provided opportunities for them to move into working with the ideas they have been able to describe, imagine, discuss, discriminate and justify?
- Have they then been able to re-appraise their discoveries, trials, compositions, etc.?

The following planning sheet has proved useful. The learning outcomes, if written in terms of what the pupils will be doing, will enable you to focus on specific actions.

YEAR GROUP?	WEEK 1	WEEK 2	WEEK 3	WEEK 4	WEEK 5	WEEK 6
Learning Outcomes						
Lesson Outline Each lesson should include elements of listening, appraising [i.e. talking about], composing, performing … How are the children being encouraged to think musically? Focus for 6 weeks:						
P.O.S.						
Resources						
Things to observe, monitor, note about pupils' musical development						

Figure 77 Chart for planning

THE MUSIC POST-HOLDER OR COORDINATOR

The historical legacy described in Chapter 1 has also affected the role of the teacher. Since music was, on the whole, seen as the preserve of a specialist, it has only been in recent years that such posts have been held by teachers who may not necessarily have the traditional musical skills recognised for the title 'specialist'. Consultancy courses have also been encouraging those with enthusiasm and motivation for music to gain understanding and support skills for the role, which now means that each school will have an appointed person, maybe with an attached allowance, to coordinate the music provision in the school. The description of such a post can vary. Some schools may want the post-holder to 'get on with it', write the school policy and be responsible for all music in the school. Other schools are breaking this traditional mould, in line with the implications of the National Curriculum, perceiving the role in broader terms. Their task is to integrate music successfully into the life of the school, helping colleagues to develop their confidence with music, and being available to support and reassure all efforts made by teachers to facilitate music in the classroom. The role, therefore, involves several different aspects.

Collaboration

Working with others to create a musical environment in the school can take many forms. Collaboration may involve paired teaching, class swaps, whole school events, shared events with other schools, engaging the assistance of parents, enlisting the support of school governors, working with others external to the school, for example, a community group, peripatetic instrumentalists and music consultants.

Besides merely organising, the role involves being able to work alongside others in ways that will ensure the provision of musical activities for the pupils. This may involve more time being spent listening and imagining a music lesson from someone else's point of view, especially if they are not as confident or as uninhibited as the post-holder.

Facilitator

The task of facilitating musical experiences for others involves being aware of how pupils learn and the ways in which musical experiences can be gained. The 'empty vessel', or more traditional didactic approach, certainly does not facilitate learners being engaged in exploration, reflecting, evaluating, personal decision making, etc., let alone in the development of the exploration of feelings, imagination or musical ways of thinking.

Since some colleagues may have had such role models for music teachers, it becomes important to help all teachers to develop and experience music for themselves in this way – for them to imagine music, to talk about their feelings about it, to experiment and so forth. All musical contributions should be valued.

Fighting the need to 'be in charge' and sticking with the 'not knowing' allows the space for the child's feeling and thinking to be experienced more fully, and places the teacher in the role of facilitator (Nelson, 1993).

Curriculum development

Curriculum development within the school should serve two masters. These are:

- to ensure progression of musical experiences for the pupils
- to provide opportunities for the teachers to develop their personal understanding

The post-holder is expected to keep abreast of general developments in the field, sharing new ideas, suggestions for resources, feedback from any conferences and such like with their staff. Curriculum development may often occur with a 'ripple affect' – information being disseminated to all staff in a range of ways, from staff meetings allocated to music, to informal chats over breaktimes.

New developments and ideas will most likely be absorbed into the overall school planning structure and may form parts of the school policy (see Chapter 5). Certainly, general staff development and INSET provision will be part of the post-holder's responsibility to coordinate. This may involve ensuring that the school governors are aware that monies need to be allocated for staff development in music. Of course, with music now being an official foundation subject (1992), there is some official funding allocated from government funds for in-service provision in music. This may be school based and offered by an outside consultant, or centrally provided via service-level agreements with local educational establishments (teachers' centres).

There should, of course, always be the opportunity for teachers to reflect on any curriculum provision. Follow-up staff meetings will enable the staff to assess how their own understanding can be translated into classroom practice. This will then have a subsequent impact on the provision of musical experiences across the school for all pupils, which should be taken into consideration.

The notion that staff should 'pause' every so often and take stock of what they are achieving is not new. The National Curriculum Council in 1992 recommended that all schools should undertake an Audit of both provision, resources, personnel and curriculum. In a similar way, a review of progress towards the goals outlined in a policy does not become unreasonable. For music it may be essential, if the confidence of the staff are to grow in relation to music teaching. Monitoring and evaluating changes in strategy, then become vital.

Managing resources

Usually it is the post-holder who is expected to deal with all aspects of music resources, from purchasing, repairing and administration, to offering suggestions for their use.

Without a whole-school strategy, decisions about what resources and where these will be located will be difficult. Will music be occurring in each classroom or in a designated 'music room' or in a central space like a hall? Maybe large musical events, which require a readily accessible central store of resources, take precedence over more regular classroom music experiences?

The role of resource management is also shared with the head teacher and the governors. It is essential that all parties are aware of how they will work together to ensure that music is taught throughout the school in accordance with the National Curriculum orders for Music.

Support

As with other curriculum areas, the post-holder should be readily approachable by staff members for assistance, guidance and general support. This may also mean being able to help teachers explore their apprehensions and anxieties about teaching music as part of a process of getting started (Nelson, 1993).

Clearly, the emphasis should be on empowerment – building on strengths already present in other class practice, and linking these with musical activities and approaches.

This part of the role may also require the post-holder to stand aside and let others not only 'have a go', but also take active responsibility for aspects of the school's music provision, such as the recorder group or the choir. Certainly, the more active models children have of adults (regardless of gender, race or culture) participating in musical activities, the greater the likelihood of music being valued and respected.

SUGGESTIONS

1 Write a brief description about the recollections you have of school music. Are your memories mostly positive or negative?

2 What kinds of information do you want to know about the children you are going to teach? How will you get this information?

3 Imagine you are planning for a small group music session. To help your classroom management strategies, make a list of all the things you would need to consider and anticipate happening.

4 Tape one of your music lessons. Listen and make a note of the kinds of questions you have asked. Analyse the results in terms of the types of questions: lower order, higher order, routine/managerial/behaviour questions.

5 Listen to the taped lesson and make a note of the verbal vocabularies used. How balanced is your use of professional, experiential and behaviour vocabularies?

6 After planning a series of lessons, with notes on things to observe about pupils, ask a colleague to join you and observe the children for those things. In what way are your observations the same or different?

FIVE

The school

Musical experiences occurring within the school need to be coordinated and integrated into the school's life, so that music can be seen as an integral part of human existence. One of the most direct ways of ensuring that this happens is by ensuring that you have a school policy.

DEVISING A SCHOOL POLICY

As with all other curriculum subjects, a music policy is required by all schools. Since it is a document that all staff can refer to for guidance and clarity, it should ideally be prepared by the staff team. Many schools begin the process with an INSET staff meeting. In this setting, all staff can begin to think about and contribute their ideas. The following key questions are useful to begin the process.

• Why have music in our school?
• What is music? What makes an activity musical?
• When and where does musical activity take place in our school?
• In what way does music provision differ between infants and juniors, for example, the use of movement and music and music in assemblies?
• Who at present provides musical opportunities in their classes?
• What musical resources do we have in the school? Where are these located? Are the access arrangements to the instruments satisfactory?
• What procedures have we implemented in other subject areas which may be applicable to enhancing the provision of the music curriculum – planning, monitoring group organisation, etc.?

The discussion from these questions can then form the starting point for a smaller working party. In this way, the staff have some ownership over at least some of the contents of the document that any working party may bring back to the group. Of course, sometimes a post-holder or a coordinator is given the task. If this is the case, whatever they come up with then needs to be shared with the whole staff with options for alteration if this is required.

Suggested contents for a primary school music policy

• Rationale for music in our school.
• The nature of music – what music involves.
• A description of when, where and how music-making occurs in school.
• Cross-curricular links/possibilities.
• Equal opportunities – equal access.
• Aims (learning outcomes, (End of Key Stage Statements)).
• Objectives (General Programme of Study).
• Teaching strategies – planning procedures/framework.
• Assessment and record-keeping suggestions (closely linked to planning).

Figure 78   Choirs involving boys

- Facilities, resources and their locations, timetabling, personnel.
- Necessary INSET required and review schedule for progress on implementing the above.

Let us now consider some of the aspects from this list in further detail.

Rationale

Why have music in our school? The reason for doing music affects all aspects of school music provision. If one is merely complying with the statutory National Curriculum requirements, there is little likelihood that musical activity in the school will have that vitality which brings enjoyment, motivation and commitment. Under these circumstances, music would certainly not be a serious contender for our time, resources,

repertoire, personnel or curriculum development; it would remain the 'Cinderella' subject.

Similarly, the way 'music' is defined will affect the many necessary decisions we need to make in order to allocate our time, resources, repertoire and personnel.

If one is a vegetarian, shopping in the supermarket would normally exclude the purchase of meat. Our value judgement has excluded some purchases. Similarly, if a school's view of music made little or no mention of music from other cultures, or indeed of the music that is 'alive' and performed within the local community by the range of different cultural groups now resident in Britain, it would hardly be surprising to find no instruments from other cultures. The value judgements inherent in the rationale are therefore very important.

Thus, the whole-school discussions about music need to establish what is meant by 'music'. The definition arrived at will determine whether pupils in your school will be more fully involved in vocal performances, than in exploring sounds and making music using a range of sound sources, or in recognising various styles of music. The definition will also influence the status given to music – is it something to help 'show-off' the school which only the talented can participate in, or is it something which all pupils are to be encouraged to experience and participate in, with the possible outcome of a 'child-centred' product rather than a 'school-centred' product?

Cross-curricular links

With a full curriculum, it is often easy to understand why teachers look for possibilities to subsume music, along with other art forms, within a given theme or topic. The danger, however, is that music may not be treated as an equal partner when such links are formed. To avoid both the integrity of music being lost and the requirements of the National Curriculum being inconsistently offered, any approach which is truly cross-curricular needs to have more than just a topic title or theme unifying it.

This means moving away from merely trying to find a song that is about the topic and a bit of theme music which might suffice. Of course, the theme or topic will be the starting point, but not solely to fit music into. How can music extend the understanding of the topic or theme? Put another way, what key concepts will the topic be highlighting that can be investigated and/or developed through the medium of sound? With these questions in mind, and using the spiral framework and planning charts, musical activities are no longer just an additional extra. Of course, even if a song is found that does 'match' the topic, using the framework provides guidance on what to do with it – identify the beat, the rhythmic phrases, the structure, the melodic shapes, the mood of the piece, the instruments that could be used to accompany it, the dynamics which will convey the meaning, etc.

Equal opportunities

Ensuring that all pupils have equal access to musical provision is clearly stated in the National Curriculum Music document. Therefore, we need to consider who our pupils are. Reference in earlier chapters has been made to learners who may bring different experiences and have different skills to offer. Areas which need consideration include:

- Do I have a gender bias when distributing instruments, for example, drums to the boys and hand bells for the girls?
- Do I have stereotyped expectations that all black children will have a natural feel for rhythm?
- Do I allow the boys to opt out of singing situations more readily than girls?
- Am I excluding pupils by the language that I use? Could visuals help?
- Am I expecting those who have separate music lessons to participate more fully or to be bored with class music?
- How am I helping those pupils who have difficulties with aspects of the music lesson to actually improve their skills? For example, is the child who never seems to be able to keep the beat dissuaded from playing or given more opportunity to practise and improve?

If your school has a separate policy on equal opportunities and/or special needs, it is important that these sections echo the sentiments and intentions suggested within them. This will ensure that the approach to these issues is consistent across all subjects.

Special educational needs

As we have all had special educational needs at some time or another, it is reasonable to assume that there will be pupils in your class who have such needs. What access can we offer them? The child who appears to have behavioural difficulties may need very structured contexts where instruments are concerned. If at all possible, try to **catch them being good** (CBG) (Montgomery, 1989), and let the reward involve having the instrument that they desire. Remember, too, that while some children may have specific difficulties learning other subjects, learning music may not involve the same obstacles. It is therefore important not to transfer expectations of poor performance into this different context, giving them more space to demonstrate their capabilities freely.

Aims and objectives

One way of interpreting the National Curriculum document is to read the End of Key Stage Statements (EOKSS) as overall learning outcomes. In effect, they are stating what it is hoped the pupils will be able to do by the age of 7 and 11. The General Programme of Study, on the other hand begins 'Pupils should be given **opportunities** . . .' followed by a list of six areas which offer a framework for the Key Stage-Specific Programme of Study. This explicitly states what essential skills, knowledge and understanding the pupils should be **taught** during each Key Stage. The somewhat artificial divisions between the Attainment Targets have now also been reduced in the Draft Proposals. The focus on action is still present; the list of activities all commence with a verb. In other words, by 'doing'

the required Programme of Study, it is expected that the pupils will be able to achieve the learning outcomes.

Resources

Many schools, beginning to consider their school music policy and general music provision in the light of the National Curriculum, will be carrying out an audit of the resources in the school which are needed for providing a music curriculum. This will include everything from instruments, records, tapes, books and music charts to personnel and accommodation.

Often, it is found that instruments are in need of repair. Any decision about repairs or new purchases should take into account how music is to be approached in the school. The rationale within the school policy should help to determine the kind of purchases made.

The view about music in the school will also affect personnel, another crucial aspect of resources. Who will be the music post-holder? What will be their responsibilities? Does the school consider it important to have a music specialist on staff, if only for a few days of the week? Will all teachers be expected to work around demands for rehearsal time for various school concerts throughout the year? Are there staff who will be able to assist at these times with complementary skills, for example, in stage management, lighting and design? (See Chapter 7.)

ASSEMBLIES

School assemblies offer a wonderful opportunity for a range of encounters with music, both active and passive. Many schools play music while children enter and leave assembly. However, more often than not, music at these times is merely being used to set the tone for the event. For those already settled in the hall, the opportunities to 'listen' are often interrupted by teachers issuing

instructions and passing comments about the behaviour of other children entering. Children can hardly be expected to take the music seriously since the adult models themselves are not in any way in a 'listening' mode.

Once settled in the hall, the actual assembly content can provide not only situations in which pupils can perform (their own and others' work),

Figure 79 Assembly with visiting musicians

but also offer the chance for children to be 'in audience'.

One of the areas in the General Programme of Study (within the area of performing and composing (AT1) across all key stages) refers to all pupils being given the opportunity to:

'**perform with others**, and develop awareness of audience, venue and occasion'
(SCAA, 1994)

This suggests that performing opportunities could be in a variety of locations (for example, outside, in a local hall or a church) and implies that an audience needs to be present. Whatever the context, if teachers are chatting to each other or parents, then the children can hardly be expected to behave differently.

In these more planned situations, assemblies can also provide the context for performances by outside groups. Listening to live music should be part of the musical experience provided by the school. An area identified under listening and

appraising (AT2) within the General Programme of Study refers to all pupils being given the opportunity to:

'**respond to and evaluate** live and recorded music including their own and others' compositions and performances'
(SCAA, 1994)

Planning for such events should be within the context of the vision in the school policy. Guest performances that bear no relation to work already being done, or which are not followed up with opportunities for discussion and possible further investigation in the classroom, may actually have a negative effect on the growing musical appetites of pupils. (Can you remember having to sit for long periods of time, without shuffling or talking, while a group performed? If, for whatever reason, your interest was not captivated, or your mind was not engaged in active listening, you learnt to tolerate the situation – but was the experience beneficial?)

LINKS WITH SECONDARY SCHOOLS

Secondary school music departments have always been faced with children arriving in year 7 from a number of contributing primary schools. Without the opportunity to meet the teachers from the various lower and middle schools, an assumption was often made that most primary schools offer only limited musical experiences to their pupils. Cloaked with almost blatant arrogance, the secondary teacher would begin a music programme that for some pupils was very new and for others was 'old hat'. This often resulted in pupils dropping music as soon as it became an option, because they had been 'switched off'; while for others who may have been 'switched on', music was pursued through to GCSE level and beyond. Recent changes in the syllabuses have contributed to greater numbers staying with music in later years.

With the arrival of the National Curriculum, a greater stress on progression and sequence across the Key Stages has been stipulated. To ensure that this can occur, there is now a greater requirement for pupil profiles and achievement records to be well maintained at every level. This will have a significant impact on all secondary departments, but particularly on music departments. Prior to the National Curriculum, assumptions could not be made about what the pupils may or may not have experienced in primary schools. Although there is now a statutory content laid down, obviously the delivery of musical experiences cannot be standardised.

Clearly, individual schools will have chosen different ways to meet the requirements. While some may have held on to a music specialist post, especially for Key Stage 2, or been able to buy in a 'music person', other schools will have been working with in-service training to see all teachers involved in taking their own class music. Whatever the process, records of pupils' musical experiences need to be well kept to ensure that the secondary teacher can indeed build on past experience (see Chapter 6). Certainly, in the future, the secondary music teacher will not be able to make the same assumptions about the experiences of their year 7 pupils. Until recently, it would have been possible to make fairly accurate predictions about which secondary schools most year 7 pupils would be attending. However, with the introduction of the Local Management of Schools (LMS), it will be less easy to predict where pupils will attend secondary school after they leave primary or middle school. This strengthens the need to provide the secondary teacher with the information they need to plan programmes which build and appropriately revisit former experiences in positive and rewarding ways.

The next chapter discusses the ways in which teachers can respond to pupils' musical utterances, and considers how pupil progress in music can be monitored.

SUGGESTIONS

1 Consider how your own school organisation either helps or hinders musical activity being promoted in the school.

2 In what ways do the 'school concerts' involve pupils in your school? Do they inhibit musical access for each child? Try to list the musical advantages for such events.

3 In what ways does your school music policy inter-link with other school policies? Can you describe what the advantages and disadvantages might be of such connections for the pupils?

4   'If the musical education children receive in schools is to be continuous and progressive, it is important not only that there should be more consultation between teachers in primary and secondary schools, but that teachers of music should prepare carefully graded schemes of work. This is especially important if more than one member of staff teaches music: in such a case, the teacher in charge of music should draw up a scheme of work after discussing the matter in detail with his or her colleagues.'
(Brocklehurst, 1962, p. 9)

Although this statement was made in 1962, consider what relevance it could have for today's context.

Monitoring musical progress

'Learning occurs not by recording information but by interpreting it. Effective learning depends on the intentions, self-monitoring, elaborations and representational constructions of the learner.'
(Gipps, 1993)

There can be little doubt about the value of monitoring pupils' work. In all subjects, the observation of pupils is an important aspect of teaching, as is the response we make to their work. We need to be able to see how the pupils are progressing with the work to ensure that each pupil's needs are being fulfilled. 'Monitoring' involves the observing and/or recording of an event or action. In an educational setting, we must evaluate this data. What, then, is assessment?

Assessment in education is the process of gathering information:

- by teachers about their pupils
- by teachers about their own teaching
- by pupils about their own progress.
  (Duncan and Dunn, 1989)

The information gathered is then able to be **evaluated** so that informed decisions can be made about:

- what specific help pupils may need (diagnosis)

- the areas in which the pupils are succeeding (monitoring)
- the next appropriate task or activity (selection)

This means that assessment should be seen as a tool to not only improve the quality of the learning provision (the lesson plan/curriculum), but also to place the 'consumer' (the pupil) at the heart of the learning context, enabling feedback on progress to be given directly to the learner and more indirectly to those removed from the situation, such as the learner's parents. In essence, assessment should help us to address three important questions:

- What do you want the pupils to learn?
- What activities and experiences promote these intentions?
- How is the evidence of learning revealed?

In music education, as with all other subjects, we need to be concerned with these questions. The National Curriculum is intended to outline what pupils should be learning (content), as well as providing some useful suggestions about what pupils 'should' be doing (actions/experiences needed) to gain musical understanding and, in more general terms, what may be expected of pupils at the end of various Key Stages.

WHAT CAN WE MONITOR?

First, we can keep a record of what we have covered in our own planning. However, merely accumulating a list of songs sung, the music

listened to or noting the musical games played, etc. will not give us information about how the pupils have developed their musical understanding. We need to be more specific.

In earlier chapters, I have described what is involved in musical understanding, stressing that it includes dealing with the actual music itself by becoming involved with the musical materials or elements and learning how they can be structured, and by being sensitive to the expressive qualities that different combinations can generate.

The UK Council for Music Education and Training (UKCMET), which became the Music Education Council (MEC) in January 1994, have prepared *NC Music Guidelines* which are being distributed to all British schools (1993). As a major force behind the changes to the NC document, they state that:

> 'Understanding music is more like knowing a person than knowing a fact, it is knowledge by direct acquaintance; knowledge of music rather than about music.'

We must, of course, plan for this 'direct acquaintance', which can happen in the contexts of singing, playing, moving, creating and directing, where listening and appraising are integral to all. This may also include reading and writing music. Our starting point is the musical materials which make up the spiral. We provide the contexts and then encourage the pupils to be sensitive to how they are being used or could be used. In these contexts, we can also observe the pupils working with the materials, combining them to make musical shapes and becoming responsive to the delights and surprises of their achievements, planned or unexpected.

Using the spiral not only helps us to plan for musical encounters, but also enables us to gradually become more focused on what understanding is being demonstrated during these encounters.

PLANNING FOR ASSESSMENT

Our planning needs to take account of the fact that the musical contexts will occur throughout all the primary school years. Within these contexts, we should be encouraging our pupils to **think and behave musically**. This will affect the musical utterances they make – be it their compositions or their discussions about music. As we develop this ability, the descriptive language used should become more refined, and pupils will begin to articulate the reasons for their musical preferences. When they do this, they are not just operating at a cognitive level, but also at a 'feeling' level. They are finding the words for their feelings as much as they are locating a language to describe the way the sounds/music appeared to them.

If we agree that one's innermost thoughts and understandings can be expressed verbally, pictorially, in sound or in gesture, then providing opportunities for young learners to investigate their feelings through different mediums is important. We all happily collect examples of pupils' drawings and paintings and watch as they gain more skill in handling the materials and organising their ideas on paper, but we also need to begin to do this with music. We can watch children's behaviour as they make and listen to music, and we can collect evidence of their discussions and their work on tape and from their symbolic notations. This requires time. We therefore need to account for this in the planning of our lessons. Have we ensured a lesson structure that will enable us to take account of the pupils' musical development?

APPLICATION OF FRAMEWORK CHECKLISTS

The charts initially discussed in Chapter 4, which appear in the appendix, can be used to assist with initial record keeping of what musical materials you have focused on and in what contexts. They can also enable you to focus on how particular musical materials are being recognised, worked with and incorporated into the vocabulary which the pupils can use in their music-making and appraising. For example, when we sing the song that has words which fit our topic, we cannot only address some or all of the materials of sound, but also begin to consider the expressive character and form of the song – the song then becomes a starting point for a musical investigation that could develop musical understanding.

Musical materials (called 'elements' in the Introductory Statements) are presented for years 1–6 in ever-increasing degrees of sophistication, plotted against the musical contexts discussed in Chapter 4 (p. 74). This reminds us that we can revisit the musical materials in all the contexts, observing pupils' behaviour as they come to know and develop their musical understanding.

If we are not clear about what we are expecting the pupils to be working at, and have not anticipated 'learning outcomes', then it will be very difficult to make our observations. For example, if we are planning a sequence of lessons which is intended to develop the pupils' understanding of 'structure', we may begin with an 'imitation' game, asking the pupils to first imitate our patterns made from body sounds. What does this activity actually entail? There are two components: the visual stimulus and the aural stimulus. Which one is going to be most important for this music lesson sequence? Setting up some examples of producing sound with the body would give the pupils a reservoir of ideas for gestures and sounds. As we observe children copying our patterns in a Simple-Simon type fashion, what can we say about their ability to copy the sounds? If, on the other hand, we remove the visual stimulus (by reproducing

sounds on a tape, or asking different children to produce the sounds coming from behind a screen), the class are solely reliant on the aural stimulus. This would involve them in the process of 'aural matching'. This may even enable some discoveries – that, for instance, a certain sound can be made in two different ways. By isolating the factors in this way, what is observable becomes more obvious, and less ambiguous. Strategies which enable the pupils to perform in twos or threes further reduce the possibility that some children are merely waiting to copy the actions of others. Observations will usually be linked to our planning.

In planning the **context** of the lesson, we focus on the actual management strategies which will facilitate the learning outcomes being achieved. In a similar way, consideration of the context suggests a need to place the lesson in the sequence of lessons. The framework we adopt for our overall planning will also help to ensure that the activities are placed in a way that allows for progression and development.

In planning the **activity** itself, we should be asking;

• What will the pupils be doing?
• Are they going to be passive or active in their engagement with the musical experience?
• Are the decisions going to be theirs or yours?
• What former skills, knowledge and experience will the pupils need to have had to achieve success at this activity?
• Can you anticipate who will have difficulty?
• How will their needs for further practice, or repetition of a skill be able to be built into the overall activity?

With these questions in mind, a list of **observable behaviour** begins to emerge. Some of this behaviour may not at first seem 'musical behaviour', for example, working in a group. However, for group music work to be developed, observing how pupils function in groups within a musical context is important information for further lesson planning. In other words, it is important to jot down what **processes** the activity will involve. Are some or all of these observable and what **procedures** will the pupils need to follow? A planned 'learning outcome' which suggests that pupils will have 'increased their understanding of harmonics' fails to give any tangible suggestions as to how you will be able to gather information about this 'understanding' in order to assess it.

This may sound like I am suggesting a return to an 'objectives' model. I am not. Teaching to objectives can severely restrict any acceptance of outcomes which have not been planned for or anticipated. I believe that flexibility is something which can be achieved only when both teacher and pupil feel secure. It would, therefore, be naïve of me to expect teachers who lack confidence in music to offer completely open-ended settings for pupils. Indeed, very experienced music teachers often find it difficult to address the issue of differentiation in classes because their structuring of the lesson has been too vague. The setting of some initial structures, however, can assist the learning and teaching process, enabling both teachers and pupils to have some sense of progress; that, for instance, Monique is 'getting better at' keeping the beat.

GATHERING INFORMATION

To collect information about the development of pupils' musical understanding, we need to observe pupils demonstrating their understanding in active music-making situations. What we will be observing is their behaviour as they create, play and listen to music. Further information can also be obtained by listening to their compositions and the way they talk about music which they have made and heard.

Observations

One of the most obvious ways of collecting information about the pupils, effective teaching strategies and learning environments is to observe pupils working at a range of activities we have set in different contexts. This means either deciding to be a 'participant observer' or a 'non-participant observer'. As the former, our interventions, comments and suggestions will inevitably alter the course of what the pupils decide to do and eventually produce. As a non-participant observer, we are more like a 'fly on the wall', and our observations will have that detachment, which as a participant observer is impossible.

Pupils can be observed in many different contexts. For instance, working in small groups:

- on group compositions (vocal, instrumental or a combination)
- rehearsing as a group for a performance of the composition
- attempting to represent sounds with symbols
- appraising/discussing/reflecting on their performance – sharing ideas
- responding to a recording of their performance, further appraisal
- responding to the interruptions and/or suggestions of others
- listening to each others' contributions
- directing/conducting each other

Working alone:

- mastering a particular technique/skill (instrumental or vocal)
- attempting to represent sounds with symbols

Figure 80   Observing a group at work

- handling and/or developing musical materials and ideas
- responding to the interruptions and/or suggestions of others
- listening to live or recorded music

Experienced classroom researchers (Walker and Adelman, 1975; Hopkins, 1985) tell us that it is much easier to observe if we draw up an observation schedule, listing the anticipated things we expect to find. This refers us back to the idea that planning is, indeed, intimately linked to assessment.

Listening

Another way in which we can collect information about how pupils are developing their musical understanding is to listen to them talking about music. This can take several forms:

- class discussions about music heard (live or recorded)
- listening to their conversations as you observe pupils working in groups

- participating with a group as another member
- tape recording a group as they work together on their own, for example, preparing a composition or working with musical ideas

We also need to listen to their compositions. As it is not always easy to attend fully when working with a whole class, the tape recorder again becomes a useful tool. Especially, by years 5–6 (Key Stage 2), pupils should be encouraged to maintain their working groups over a period of time. This will allow a teacher to record compositions by the same group over several months. From this it is possible to see how their musical ideas are developing:

- Are they repeatedly using the same materials, structures and ideas, or is there a noticeable development?
- In what ways are the compositions changing?
- Can you relate any changes detected to the input of musical ideas arising from recent lessons or directly suggested by yourself?

Track 72

Listen to Track 72. Four year 6 pupils have had the opportunity to compose a piece of music with instruments of their choice. They were also asked to devise some form of 'notation' to represent their composition.

Figure 81   Group performance

Over previous weeks, this group had been working on beginnings and endings, dynamics and contrasts. Listen to the first 'performance' of their composition, in which some of these aspects have been incorporated.

Several weeks later, the same group was asked to perform their composition in assembly. They returned to their 'notation' and began rehearsing. I have transcribed part of their dialogue which preceded their final version.

Child A: No, I liked the way we all came in one by one.

Child B: Yes, I started and then you came in on the shaker and . . .

Child C: It is just like we wrote it down, look . . . (points to their score)

Child A: OK, but I wasn't going bang bang bang bang bang! (makes sounds)

Child B: I remember, you made shorter sounds before . . . sort of something like this . . . (demonstrates on tambourine)

Child D: Didn't I get louder as I went up?

Child C: How many times did we do it through? I can't remember.

Child B: Yeah, we'd better decide that . . . three or four times?

Child D: What about stopping one by one so there is only one sound left? Why don't you stop first because you started, and then you (points to Child C) and then me and you will look at each other and finish together. OK?

Teacher: Do you all know when to get louder and quieter?

Child D: Miss, that's easy, he leads, but they have to listen to me too.

Track 73

Now listen to their final version (Track 73). How successful do you think the group has been at remembering what they did before and working together as a group?

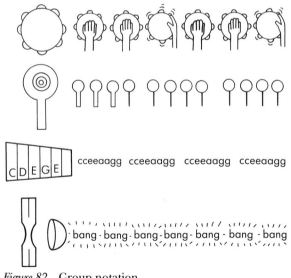

Figure 82   Group notation

Here we are potentially involved in making qualitative judgements about their musical **products**. As the paintings, stories, objects, etc. that children create are put on display, commented upon and valued, so too we must remember not to shy away from valuing both their musical behaviour (observed as they are in the process of music-making), and their actual compositions and performances. The UKCMET document (1993) suggests 'we can demonstrate our own valuing of music by the way we respect and attend to the music of children and others'. (Remember my reference to assemblies in Chapter 5.)

MAKING JUDGEMENTS

When we observe or listen to children working with music, we are inevitably involved in making judgements. Comments such as, 'That's good, I like the way you have used the triangle there', are a personal judgement prompted by your own response and sensitivity to the expressive qualities in the music. At this moment, we would be using what I referred to in Chapter 5 as 'experiential vocabulary'. When we then notice that the triangle player is having difficulty playing a rapid pattern, our comment may then require us to use 'behavioural vocabulary': 'Is there a way of holding the triangle that would make it easier?'; or 'professional vocabulary': 'What could be changed so that Simon didn't find that pattern so difficult to play?' (maybe reducing the tempo?).

We are also called upon to make judgements when we evaluate pupils' performances. To provide information that can be fed back to the learner, that will help us to plan the next step in the journey, and enable us to record in some way the bench marks that have been reached, we are again faced with the need to make judgements. However, making judgements in music education is problematic. The Music Advisers' National Association (MANA) in 1986 stated:

'If music education is concerned with teaching pupils to discriminate, to be able to decide for themselves, on critical grounds, what is worthwhile, it should concentrate particular attention on approaches to assessment which begin with the individual's response in a musical encounter.'
(MANA, 1986, p. 8)

Therefore, how does one judge a pupil's individual response to a musical encounter, since that response is of a very personal nature? What if the pupil's judgement is not in accordance with that of the teacher's? Education, the arts and evaluation are all bound up with values. Children's and teachers' values are all implicated in any attempt to pass judgements about educational attainment, which must be seen as the thrust of any National Curriculum document full of 'Attainment Targets'.

The Gulbenkian Foundation in their report 'The Arts in Schools' (1982) argued that judgements in the arts are to an extent, founded on feeling and intuition:

'The arts enable us to assert ideas and judgements which we may recognise collectively to be true but which cannot be proven in other ways, through empirical experiment for example. Intuitive judgement must be recognised as a legitimate element in evaluating this work in schools. Attempts to make the arts accountable by submitting them to forms of assessment which properly belong elsewhere may actually make them appear wanting by looking for inappropriate forms of "proof".'

The end of Key Stage statements describe:

'the types and range of performance which pupils should characteristically demonstrate by the end of each Key Stage. The statements are designed to help teachers judge the extent to which their pupils' attainment relates to this expectation'
(SCAA, 1994)

The former Non-statutory guidelines are still however valuable. In order to make those judgements, it will be necessary to:

- decide what evidence is required (from, for example, a performance, composition, a piece of writing, pupil discussion, etc.);

- decide if further criteria are required (referring to the EOKSS);
- discuss those judgements with other teachers to ensure consistency.'

(NCC, 1992)

INVOLVING PUPILS IN ASSESSMENT

In other subjects, you may already be involving your pupils in making assessments about their work and asking them to begin to record this. In music, the same opportunities exist for pupil participation in gathering information about their work. A wall chart will enable pupils to record what instruments they have used.

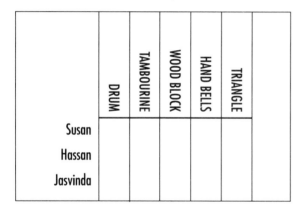

	DRUM	TAMBOURINE	WOOD BLOCK	HAND BELLS	TRIANGLE	
Susan						
Hassan						
Jasvinda						

Figure 83 Example of a wallchart of instruments played by children in a class

For those children who abuse this chart by seeking to accumulate ticks, a week without instruments because they have played them all, will soon indicate that the chart should be valued as a record to ensure each child does, indeed, get an opportunity to play every instrument.

Asking pupils to write a brief description of what they did during their music lesson will also give you not only a record of their perceptions, but also a potential insight into their developing attitude towards music.

Figure 84 opposite shows a record card which I

have used.

Since musical judgement is such a personal thing, I have found that asking pupils to respond to the music composed and/or performed by others is a useful way to gather information about how they are developing their own understanding about musical materials, expressive qualities and form. It should also be noted that the NSG make the recommendation that pupils should also be involved in making judgements about their own performances. This is also part of Attainment Target 2 (listening and appraising). Here I have adapted an idea from a language lesson I observed, where pupils were asked to respond to another child's story.

As you glance through their responses, do any patterns emerge? This should not surprise you because what you are noticing is that there may be a consensus about particular aspects of the composition. It is this same consensus that raises some music to 'top of the pops'. Especially where compositions have clear boundaries at the beginning, (such as 'a journey', or 'an animal') it will be revealing to see whether those in the audience shared similar perceptions about what the 'journey' or 'animal' was. If many of the pupils suggest a similar title, then it is safe to claim that the piece managed to 'communicate' something that was perceived and shared. This will have been due to the powerful effect of the expressive qualities and structure – in other words, the way the musical materials were used and performed together.

FOR USE BY THE PERFORMER(S):

NAME: **DATE:**   **YEAR GROUP:**

Name two things you liked doing:

Name two things you didn't like doing:

Name two things you would like more time on:

Name two things you would like to get better at doing:

Describe two musical discoveries you made:

Name two things you really enjoyed about the lesson:

Say who you enjoyed working with and why:

Figure 84   Personal evaluation of music-making

FOR USE BY THE AUDIENCE:

NAME: **DATE:**

Describe two things you liked:

Describe two things that you didn't like:

Did you hear any repeated patterns? If so, what instrument was playing it?

Describe one thing you thought could have been improved:

Describe HOW you would suggest improving it:

Suggest your own title for the piece you heard and say why you would give this title:

Figure 85   Personal evaluation of music heard

Whatever procedure you adopt in your classroom to monitor the musical development of each pupil, never let the information gathered be an end in itself. The data we have should help us to provide musical activities which will meet the needs of our pupils. We will be able to gradually build on their growing expertise and understanding, in a very similar way to that of our own changing perceptions and interpretations.

OFSTED inspectors will also be interested in seeing evidence of how the pupils are developing musically. Records of pupil's comments, your own observation notes, their notations and recordings of pupil's work will be valuable information to share with an inspector. Chapter 7 considers the range of resources needed to develop and enhance children's musical experiences.

SUGGESTIONS

1 'Estimating a child's performance in, and contribution to, a large group activity requires very careful observations. Whether or not this can be successfully undertaken by the class teacher during normal curriculum time is very doubtful.' (Plummeridge, 1991, p. 86)

   In view of the suggestions made in this chapter, discuss this statement with your colleagues. What conclusions can be drawn about the teaching strategies used in other areas which could be adopted in music lessons?

2 Make a list of those aspects of a musical activity you feel you would have no difficulty observing. Consider ways to incorporate this into your music planning.

3 Discuss point (2) with your colleagues; maybe they feel they have strengths in different areas? How could you begin to share the monitoring of each pupil's musical progress?

4 If at all possible, observe pupils in a musical situation led by another colleague. Afterwards, compare your findings. In what ways did the observed pupil behaviour match the teacher's intended outcomes for the lesson?

5 When you set a group off to work on their own musical composition, tell them you want to tape record their discussion, so that you can learn how they are thinking out the problems posed. Take time to listen to the tape of their dialogue, making notes about the ideas individuals were bringing. Were there any surprises?

SEVEN

Resources

As mentioned in Chapter 5, resourcing for the music curriculum needs to take account of any major policy statements made. Indeed, the way music is viewed in the school will determine how resources will be viewed. There are many different kinds of resources to be considered.

PUPILS' EXPERIENCES

Chapters 2 and 3 drew attention to the fact that young pupils will already have a resource of musical experience which should be developed. Some will already have a repertoire of nursery rhymes and songs, not always of English origin. Some may be very responsive to a salsa or reggae beat, while others may prefer a range of raga tone scales and melodic intervals which are not so readily captured in traditional English music. Of course, some children may arrive with a more arid musical experience by comparison, but with a well-defined aural memory for advertising jingles and phrases heard repeatedly from the television. On the other hand, a few pupils in your class may bring very different abilities which will require specific provision such as those pupils with hearing, sight or physical impairments. Their musical responsiveness should be catered for, as they also need to be given the opportunities stipulated in the National Curriculum.

Whatever their previous musical experience, teachers must try to tap into these accumulated understandings, providing opportunities for children to demonstrate their acquired skills. These are more likely to be manifested in open-ended situations, where the children are not inhibited by the rules they are expected to follow, such as playing an instrument in only one way. Opportunities need to be provided so that we can consciously tap into this store of music, for instance, by asking the children to sing or tap out their favourite pattern. Those pupils with limited English will soon grasp what is expected, and will then feel that their contributions, too, will be valued.

By Key Stage 2, most learners will have had two or more years in the British school system. One could expect to find records from previous classes on their experiences in music (see Chapter 6). While records give an account of the opportunities provided and the activities encountered, the notes which indicate the kind of musical behaviour observed will be one of the most valuable starting points for the next teacher.

With the pupils come parents and families. Some may include musicians who would be willing to assist in the musical opportunities the school wanted to provide for the pupils. Naturally, if music is seen as a mere 'add-on' in the midst of an already crowded curriculum timetable, it is likely that the opportunities in the immediate community will not be perceived, let alone incorporated into the life of the school.

STAFF MEMBERS

As adults, we are likely to have a wide repertoire of musical experiences at our disposal. Some of us may have lived in foreign countries or have partners from other cultures, which may mean that staff have an interesting music collection at home. Others may, at one time, have learnt an instrument themselves, which they still retain. Certainly, it is sometimes easy to pass over our own experience in the light of a member of staff who is known to be 'musical'.

Providing opportunities where staff can contribute their likes and dislikes, where individual tastes are accepted, is no different from the value it is hoped we could place on an individual child's musical contribution.

Elsewhere, reference has been made to the fact that class teachers are more often in a better position to be able to assess pupil needs and understand pupils' progress than a visiting teacher who only sees the class for one lesson a week. It is exactly this kind of resource that should be regularly tabled as an important asset.

In 1978, the HMI in their *Primary Report* recommended the model of the generalist class teacher who is supported by a curriculum leader or coordinator (also referred to as the post-holder). As discussed in Chapter 4, the coordinator/post-holder may or may not be a music specialist – often being able to play the piano for assembly was enough to qualify for the post! The role of coordinator has become familiar in every curriculum area. Now, skills on the keyboard do not always imply evidence of the necessary communication skills needed when working with colleagues who lack musical confidence – often an enthusiastic generalist will be a less intimidating music post-holder.

The school may have a tradition of visiting instrumental teachers. Depending on local arrangements, these may be still available or may no longer be on offer. Clearly, where schools have managed to maintain such tuition, the school could seek to make wider use of the music personnel who visit the school on a regular basis. The coordinator should look for ways to integrate these tutors, especially if the school wants to promote the image of music for all. There are known cases where this kind of musical input has held more status with the pupils than actual class music lessons. What is this saying to pupils about musical encounters generally and musical participation in particular?

TIME

Generally, the time allocated to music in the school will reflect the views of music expressed in the overall policy document:

- How much time is set aside for music in the infant school?
- Does this change as pupils move into the junior school?
- Is music indeed a timetabled slot, necessary because of the use of a particular space, or the movement and sharing of musical instruments?
- What time is set aside across the school year for music INSET with the staff, or for the coordinator to work collaboratively with colleagues?
- What time is made available for certain children to be released for private lessons, or for rehearsals for school events? Here the emphasis on 'process' or 'products' will become evident, as certain activities have precedence over others, thereby indicating priorities and values.

ACCOMMODATION

- What facilities does the school have for whole-class activities, group activities and individual work?
- Are teachers willing to accommodate music lessons in classrooms which may mean both being disturbed by and creating a disturbance to others?
- Where a special room is allocated to music, is this readily accessible for all?
- Are satisfactory spaces available for small groups to practise, or are children to be allowed to play in the corridors, cloakrooms, etc.?
- Are all the instruments located centrally, or distributed across 'floors' on trolleys, or to be found in various combinations in classrooms?
- How are the rest of the teaching resources made accessible to staff? Are they kept locked up for use by the visiting teacher only?
- Is the one high-quality audio system fixed in a location that restricts its use?

EQUIPMENT

Under this heading the following can be included:

- instruments (tuned and untuned)
- audio playback and recording facilities (including listening posts and headphones)
- electronic instruments (rhythm machines, keyboards, etc.)
- a listening library of tapes, records (possibly CDs)
- stands (table stands and expanding music stands)
  (Books and teaching materials are mentioned under repertoire)

Whether these are part of the school's equipment list will again be determined by the kind of musical opportunities the school plans to offer. Points for consideration when purchasing resources:

- Are the instruments:
  - made from different materials (wood, metal, plastic, gut, natural fibres, etc.)?
  - able to be played in different ways (tapping, scraping, shaking, blowing, plucking, etc.)?
  - providing a spread of pitched sounds (that is, not all within the soprano range)?

Figure 86 Grouping instruments

  - varied in size (suitable to be handled by the age range in the school)?
- Is there a variety of different type of beaters, brushes, etc., so that pupils can experiment with different effects?
- Will a range of instruments be readily accessible, for example, on a sturdy music trolley?
- Is there a variety of musical instruments from other cultures?

- What kind of electronic instruments could be incorporated (see pp. 104–9)?
- Do existing audio playback facilities enable a high-quality sound reproduction to ensure the learners have access to superior listening opportunities?
- Will the location of musical activities affect the security arrangements?
- Is an extension lead necessary to give more flexibility to the location of the equipment in classrooms?
- Are there procedures in place for the recording of radio/TV music programmes?
- Is there satisfactory storage space for pupils' books accompanying such programmes?
- Will situations arise where you might want to record pupils' work? What might these be?
- Would you allow pupils the opportunity to record their own performances – if so, how 'precious' will the equipment become? (You can now get very good hand-held recording machines the size of a Walkman which pupils could use on their own.)

For group work, and to avoid the noise factor, a listening post or junction box can be used. Readily purchased or made up by a local audio supplier, a listening post is plugged into the headphone socket at the back of the tape recorder or keyboard. The sound is then divided and can be sent out to three or four headphone sockets.

For pairs of students working together, a two-way socket can be used, into which two sets of headphones can be plugged. This means that a group can be working on a musical activity in one part of the room, while the rest of the class are involved in other work, not necessarily of a musical nature.

Figure 88   Children working in groups and individually, with headphones

- What criteria for selecting listening repertoire will you use (see below)?
- Stands: two different types are used for different musical situations. Small desk stands are useful for a class performing its own and other's arrangements and compositions, and can be used by pupils sitting at desks playing recorders. The adjustable expanding stands offer the recorder player the opportunity to stand while playing, can also be used by vocal groups and will be invaluable for any ensemble

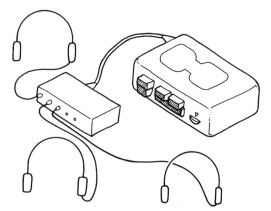

Figure 87   Listening post or junction box

and orchestral group work. Without the personnel to offer, say, orchestral opportunities, certain types of instruments and instrumental scores may not be needed. On the other hand, if a teacher is willing to set up a recorder group, tutor books, suitable repertoire and stands will be required. Should the school provide the recorders or will parents be expected to purchase these? What are the implications for equal opportunities with this latter decision?

REPERTOIRE

This covers four basic areas:

- singing
- listening
- playing
- productions/shows

There are many different ways of approaching the selection of repertoire. Whatever your criteria, it is important that the pupils are foremost in your mind, as it is for them that you will be making the purchase. Having knowledge of their interests, their musical skills and their previous musical repertoire will guide you in your selection (another justification for keeping music profiles on pupils).

The following points will be useful for consideration:

Vocal material

- Is the content of the song appropriate for the age group intended?
- How does the melodic line move around (in great leaps, steps, across a range)?
- Is the piece within the vocal range of your pupils?
- Do you find it musically interesting (maybe someone in the shop could sing or play it for you)? Will the musical style sustain the interest of your pupils?
- Is there an accompanying cassette?
- How does the idiom of this piece contrast with other songs taught? How will this piece add to their own musical repertoire?

- Will this piece offer opportunities for pupils to direct/conduct?
- Does this piece offer opportunities for a class accompaniment?

Vocal range: many believe that young children can more easily sing in the lower part of their vocal range, and select material accordingly. However, children can and should be encouraged to sing in the 'head voice', not just their chest voices. Research by Moor and Kemp (1991) and Cleall (1970) suggests the range should be D to D'.

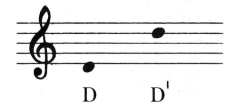

Figure 89 Vocal range D – D'

Generally the chest voice is used for talking, and the head voice is engaged when children sing in the middle to higher ends range. Therefore, to engage the head voice in singing is to also engage a different part of the perceptual senses. Laurence (1991) suggests:

'. . . the advantage of developing the head tone in children lies in its direct connection to the "inner ear" . . . the singer actually hears the note she or he is producing more clearly than in the chest tone and this develops intonation skills more quickly.'
(p. 64)

Playing material

- What skills are required? Reading bass and treble clef? Using two beaters? Being able to manipulate complicated rhythmic patterns? What technical skills will this music demand? Will this piece stretch their skills in a realistic manner?
- How many of the class/group will be excluded because of the demands of this piece? Could I make the necessary alterations to include others?
- How will this piece extend their own musical frameworks? Is it in a different style to previous work? Is it an arrangement of a familiar tune? Will it sustain their musical interest?
- Are you thinking 'performance' piece or 'study' piece?
- Can I incorporate any new players into the music group with this piece, thereby involving more pupils in this music-making experience?
- Will this piece offer opportunities for pupils to direct/conduct?

Listening

- Is all the music of a particular type/genre? How could this be extended?
- Do you have examples of music from other cultures played on authentic instruments?
- Do you cover the range of musical eras implied in the National Curriculum? Have you also got a selection of music by twentieth-century composers of both sexes?
- Is there a selection of instrumental and vocal styles, for example, for folk, opera, spiritual, pop, choral, musical hall, madrigal, a cappella, barber shop, children's voices, adult voices, from other countries, jazz cantatas, specially composed vocal works for children?
- Do you have examples from which different aspects of the spiral could be extracted and contrasted, for example, a piece played on clavichord and then by contrast on a synthesiser?
- Do you have examples of music composed, performed and conducted by women as well as men?

Productions/shows

- What is the purpose of this event, to impress parents and governors and/or to offer pupils an experience of this kind of performance?
- All the questions raised under vocal material should also be considered here.
- How many children will this involve? Will this be across the age range of the school, or really only for a particular year group?
- What possibilities are there for additional performances, which other teachers might be able to work on, for example, dance, mime, gymnastics?
- Are other staff members willing to participate in the production, both as performers and as members of the production team?
- What amount of rehearsal time will be required? Can you realistically afford this time, especially if there are vocal and instrumental groups to prepare? Will the rest of the staff willingly cooperate with the possible interruptions to classwork?

INCORPORATING ELECTRONIC EQUIPMENT

Many pupils will have electronic music-making equipment at home. It is worthwhile considering how this expertise and skill can be valued and incorporated into class music-making. Some children may have found the equipment frustrating because of their own limited musical framework, while others may have developed their musical understanding to quite sophisticated levels, persevering and taking the time to make all manner of discoveries about the opportunities the equipment may provide.

Most electronic equipment can offer some or all of the following:

- rhythm patterns
- sound/timbral options
- stylistic extensions
- sequencing facilities
- composition opportunities
- assistance with introducing harmony/chord work

Many teachers have managed to give me reasons why electronic keyboards were too difficult to include in their lessons – an extension lead could not be found, or the keyboard dominated the sound in the room, for example. Both can be solved (see Fig. 88). It is my belief that well thought-out activities can make keyboards an excellent group focus for some very intense musical investigations, discoveries and processes.

Applying the spiral framework

The spiral framework becomes a helpful starting point when considering the use of keyboards. I shall use it to review some of the possibilities that I have used with my pupils.

Beat

Most keyboards will have a beat/rhythm section. Whether there is the possibility to alter the tempo will depend on the age of the machine. Ask the pupils to listen to the selection offered by the machine, to discover three style patterns which have a different beat or feel to them. (**NB** track 2 of the tape accompanying this book.) All in the group must agree on the patterns. Pupils could be asked to accompany the pattern with a suitable classroom instrument. Decisions about matching sound qualities and styles will need to be made. Certainly, the pupils would be demonstrating their own understanding of these issues, given that many may have a far broader listening repertoire than ourselves.

Rhythm

Assuming it is possible to change the tempo, ask either the class, or more suitably, a group of children, to try to decode the rhythm pattern for a particular style. The charts below, taken from a keyboard tutor book (Butler and Barker, 1978) show how the patterns are built up.

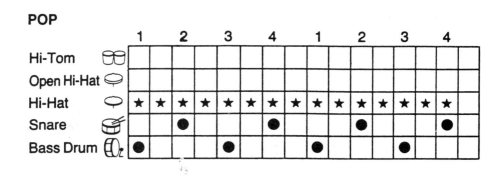

DISCO

Notice how by changing the Bass Drum to sound on every beat of the bar the same rhythm adopts a *Disco* feel.

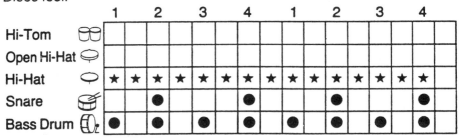

ROCK

Again, altering the Bass Drum while leaving the Hi-Hat and Snare the same, changes the rhythm to a *Rock* type.

Figure 90 Rhythm patterns

The pupils in this problem-solving activity will be using a range of skills and demonstrating them as they decode a pre-set pattern. The sounds heard will need to be identified and labelled. Another group could then try to translate the deciphered grid (the musical score) on to classroom instruments or represent the pattern with vocal sounds. Experiments could be carried out to see what happens when the tempo is increased. These grids can also be used to help the group design their own drum programme from the percussion pads which may be on the keyboard.

Choosing a rhythm style and an appropriate tempo to accompany a class song will be another group task. The pupils will have to sing the song over to themselves, seeking to find a consensus about the 'best-matched' style for this song. In the process, the pupils may discover that a change in rhythm, while fitting the actual pulse of the song, may completely alter the 'feel' of the song. The discussion arising from this certainly engages more than just listening and appraising skills!

Structure

Planning and designing a sequence of sounds creates a structure. Using a particular structure will determine the order and sequence of sounds. Therefore, with these two approaches in mind, at the simplest level, pupils could be asked to design a sequence of sounds that is 'regularly interrupted'. Whether the pupils seek to interrupt their sound with a drum fill or rhythm break, or with a completely different sound quality, is entirely their choice. Asking them to explain the reasons for their choice will encourage the pupils to think about what they were intending to express, what effect they were hoping to communicate and what feeling they had decided to try to provoke in the listener.

On the other hand, a particular structure could be selected. For example, a question and answer form can be used as the basis to allow pupils to make selections from the large range of sounds available.

Dynamics

Some keyboards offer the opportunity to alter the balance of volume between the right and left hands (melody line and chords). Others simply have one volume control.

Blending electronically generated sounds with acoustic sounds is a delicate matter, and involves great sensitivity and skill. Pupils can be offered the opportunity to develop these skills at an early age, sharpening both their aural awareness and musical sensitivities. If it has been agreed to conclude a group composition with a diminuendo (a gradual decrease in loudness), the keyboard player will, of necessity, have to match the group sounds. Their ability to play and control the volume may result in another group member operating the dynamic knob. Experience has led me to believe that this is more difficult than one would at first think, because the player is not in control of how the sound is generated – it is not like the physical movement required to gradually reduce the tambourine sound.

Tempo

Most machines will have a tempo button. With ready-made sound patterns, organised in different styles, such as rock, funk, jazz and disco, it is possible to test out the effect of changes in tempo. This can help pupils think about the general consequences of tempo, not just on the 'feel' of the music, but for the players. A young triangle player begins to have difficulty if the tempo requires movements that are too rapid. This can result in some children finding more appropriate ways of holding the instrument, while for others it can be time to 'give up' in disgust.

Altering the the tempo when the 'chord' mode has been selected can invite other possibilities. Using a matching task (similar to that mentioned under *Beat*), pupils can experiment with reducing the speed of an instantly played chord. For example, if a 'country style' is chosen, the keyboard has the facility to play that chord, organised in the style found in country music. With tuned percussion on hand, pupils in small groups can be directed to work out the sequence of notes for the chord, and then to order those notes 'in the style of . . .'. In this way pupils make discoveries for themselves about harmony that in the past could have been handled by a teacher in a very didactic manner. Prompted with leading, higher order questions on a work card, a group of, for example three to four children can sustain discussion and focused investigation for ten to twenty minutes. I am always surprised at the quality of their discussions and the way pupils have reported the processes they went through. (This is most likely going to be a Key Stage 2 activity. However, some six- to seven- year-olds will be able to do this, too, and should not be dissuaded – our job is to extend and develop musical understanding for all, which does involve offering different opportunities for differing abilities.)

Timbre

Keyboards usually provide the player with the opportunity to select from a range of 'instrument' names, the sounds they wish to play. Smaller keyboards may not have the options to 'manipulate the sounds' in ways larger, more sophisticated keyboards can provide, which often makes the sounds seem unrealistic and phoney. However, as a sound source for classroom accompaniments and compositions, they are a far cry from the piano sound.

The range of timbres available on the drum pads can also prove a valuable addition to the percussion section. Pupils can be asked to decide on an instrumental sound for a song accompaniment. What were their reasons for choosing that instrument? Was it the feeling of the song they wanted to re-create with the tone of the sound? After all 'Twinkle, twinkle little star' would sound different played on a cello, rather than on bells!

Pitch
Sometimes when a chime bar set has been broken up, so that individual children have the notes for a chord sequence, it may be impossible to find another tuned instrument with a full set of notes. A keyboard can then be another instrument

which will provide that facility. While some children play the chords, can the others work out which notes sound good in combination, and which appear to clash? What can they notice about the notes?

Because a selection of instruments is available on the keyboard, pupils have the opportunity to listen to sounds that may be much lower or higher in pitch than can be offered by classroom instruments. For those with hearing difficulties, the provision for greater extremes to be heard may be quite significant.

MIDI LINKS

'Midi' stands for musical instrument digital interface. Put simply, this facility (not available on all keyboards) enables linkage between several keyboards and/or a computer. Information from one keyboard is sent as digital information down a cable to another keyboard. Some years ago I was able to make use of a keyboard that had small-

sized keys, but a wonderful range of sounds, by linking it to a keyboard with larger-sized piano keys. Although I was playing the larger keys, I had access to the greater range of sound sources from the smaller keyboard. Midi cables are required when linking a music keyboard to a computer.

COMPUTERS

With a rapidly changing market, it would be impossible to recommend specific computers or software packages. However, several general points can be made which will be useful if you are interested in this area.

• Many computers boast music facilities, but do check on the presence of a 'sound chip', and, indeed, on the quality of this sound chip. In the mid-1980s, a certain computer company was advocating sound possibilities, but there was no sound chip in the computer, which limited the kind of facilities the software written for it could offer.

• There are many software packages. When considering a purchase, be very clear about:

– Why you want to have a computer-music facility?
– Who will be using it?
– What additional extras will also be needed to make full use of the facilities, for example, keyboard, midi cables, small mixing desk, four-track recorder?
– The likely time demands, both for yourself and for your pupils.
– The kinds of musical demands being made on the pupils, for example, some packages ask children mere memory-recall type questions, which they have to answer via the computer keyboard, not a musical keyboard; some require the pupils to make aural discriminations (from a poor sound chip) and

again enter their responses via the computer keyboard; still others provide pupils with no opportunities to manipulate sounds for themselves, to try things out or to re-arrange patterns.

Caution needs to be used, and if in doubt a music education consultant who is familiar with microtechnology and music in the classroom should be approached. Computers can prove very useful tools in the classroom, but teachers need to be very clear about what additional musical opportunities they are going to provide their learners.

- Will they offer extension in composition work?
- How will you monitor all the pupils' progress?
- How will you ensure that every pupil has the opportunity to work on the computer?
- Will there be a specific 'music-designated' computer, or time in the week when the classroom computer will be used only for music?

- Is the classroom computer a suitable computer for this purpose?

While it is easy to say that the selection of resources is determined by the amount of money available, clearly how music is perceived by the staff will also affect the prioritising of funds. Some schools may decide to invest in orchestral instruments that only a few pupils can use, but which will ensure status for the school. Others may decide to invest in classroom instruments to ensure that at each stage in the school there is a supply of instruments in a satisfactory condition. Of course, with the resources in place, it is vital that there is a way of thinking about how these could be used by pupils.

Whatever the motivation behind your selection of resources, there should be some explicit mention of your reasoning in the rationale of your school policy.

SUGGESTIONS

1 Reflect on the following statements, and relate the themes back to your own school circumstances. What are the areas of agreement, disagreement, similarity or difference?

'Given the cost of good classroom percussion instruments, it can be tempting to stock the percussion trolley with home-made ones. Unfortunately, many physically outlive their period of musical use. A yoghurt pot containing gravel does not sound as interesting as a maraca. Once its maker has forgotten the excitement of assembling it, it is best disposed of. A yoghurt pot can be a very boring instrument to play. And when you become bored, you stop listening and playing degenerates to become mere mechanical action.'
(Mills, 1991, p. 32)

'Music is a whole-school matter. All staff need to be involved in teaching it. All staff need to be involved with children making it. All staff need to share a common understanding and attitude to music. Rooms, equipment and the sound environment should be managed on a whole-school basis.'
(Glover and Ward, 1993, p. 16)

2 Highlight aspects of this chapter to raise at a staff meeting. Be able to justify your selection of key points chosen for discussion.

3 The spiral framework was briefly applied to the use of electronic keyboards in schools. Take another aspect of 'resources' and work through the spiral in a similar manner. Then relate your suggestions to the lists in the appendix. Can your suggestions be linked to a specific year group?

Contents of tape

SIDE A, TRACKS 1–9, DURATION

1 After a pulse with a bass drum, the following
music will be phased in:
Irish
Latin American
Greek
English folk
Indian
pop music
baroque music

2 Feeling the number of beats in the bar:
reggae
waltz
march
jazz

3 a) Chanting in church.
b) Simple 'child-like' percussion band – no
pulse recognisable.
c) Wind music.

4 Repeating 3(b) example above with the
addition of pulse = organisation.

5 Word sentences spoken.

6 'Polly put the kettle on' (three examples),
then examples 1 and 3 repeated.

7 a) Say names with a clap on the beat.
b) Clap the syllables against the pulse.

8 Sounds of wood block, agogo, triangle,
shaker (that is, long/short sounds).

9 Sounds of kazoo, claves, drum, shaker
(played in sequence twice).

TRACKS 10–19, STRUCTURE

10 Two short examples – one more 'march-like'
than the other (due not only to the pulse, but
also the use of instrumental timbres, etc.).

11 Three spoken examples with the pulse/feel
played over the top:
a) 'Grand old Duke of York'
b) 'Polly put the kettle on'
c) 'Jack and Jill went up the hill'

12 Two played examples on wind or string
instruments (to show phasing/breathing);

'Mary had a little lamb' and 'Jack and Jill
went up the hill'.

13 'Frère Jacque' clearly showing 'echo'.

14 'Question and answer' sung solo with chorus
(to the tune of 'London Bridge') with words.

15 'Hot cross buns' sung with accompaniment
played twice.

16 Short phrases linked in a short composition
in the style of a gavotte:
A B A C A A

17 Theme of 'Baa baa black sheep' with
    variations:
    a) straight
    b) back-to-front
    c) transposed
    d) different pulse/metre
    e) Chinese version

18 Taking four rhythmic patterns:
    a) played in 1-2-3-4 order
    b) played in 4-2-3-1 order
19 Three different versions of some sound-
    groups (see figure 21).

TRACKS 20–24, DYNAMICS

20 Take example 18(b) and add dynamics.
21 'Frère Jacque' (arrangement from Nurture
    pack):
    a) with no dynamics
    b) with dynamics to emphasise 'echo' form
22 'Train is a-coming' (vocals with arrangement)
    demonstrating a train at first in the distance,
    gradually coming closer and becoming
    louder as the station is approached. Then
    gradually decreasing volume as it moves off
    into the distance again.
23 a) Ballet piece showing contrasts of loud and
       quiet.
    b) Composition that gradually becomes
       louder.
24 Excerpt from the 'Rite of Spring: Dance of
    the Adolescents'.

TRACKS 25–29, TEMPO

25 'If you're happy and you know it'
    (vocal + accompaniment):
    a) normal 'happy' tempo
    b) slower 'not so happy' tempo
    c) happy tempo again
26 Song (vocals + accompaniment) 'I can stretch
    up'.
27 a) A maraca gradually getting faster.
    b) A triangle gradually getting faster.
    c) Claves gradually increasing tempo.
28 (See Track 22) 'Train is a-coming'
    (instrumental) demonstrating a train at first
    in the distance, gradually coming closer and
    becoming slower and louder as the station is
    approached. Then gradually increasing
    tempo while decreasing volume as it moves
    off into the distance again.
29 March-like composition (c.f. Track 10):
    a) at an inappropriate speed for a march feel
    b) at a more appropriate speed

TRACKS 30–34, TIMBRE

30 The sounds of:
    a) recorder
    b) woodblock
    c) tambourine
    d) giro
31 Repeat Track 30 (same order).
32 'In the darkness':
    a) without vocals, arrangement with sampled
       string sounds
    b) without vocals, arrangement with sampled
       brass sounds

c) without vocals, arrangement with percussion

33 'In the darkness':

a) with vocals accompanied with a plucked string on melody

b) with vocals accompanied with a bowed string on melody

34 a) A version of 'The elephants' as influenced by Saint-Saëns.

b) A version of 'The hens' as influenced by Saint-Saëns.

B SIDE TRACKS 35–42, PITCH

35 Father bear–baby bear (low sound–high sound) twice.

36 a) Father–mother–baby bear (low–middle–high sound) twice.

b) Reverse of (a) – once only.

37 Baby bear on violin – father bear on double bass – mother bear on cello (twice).

38 a) Repeat Track 37.

b) First two phrases of 'Hot cross buns'.

39 a) Repeat Track 38(b).

b) Third phrase of 'Hot cross buns' (played twice).

40 Whole version of 'Hot cross buns' played twice.

41 a) Play C C# D D# E F F# G.

b) Play C E G separately.

c) Play chord of C (CEG together) (the happy chord).

d) Add vocals to separated chord C E G.

e) Sing vocals 'Mic-hael row' while the C E G notes are played.

f) Play C E♭ G as separate notes.

g) Play as chord.

h) CEG played separately.

i) CEG played as a chord.

j) 'Hot cross buns' sung (solo voice) with the C chord appearing on the beat of every bar.

k) 'Hot cross buns' is sung again (solo voice) using the F chord played where appropriate.

42 'Four big steps and five little steps'.

TRACKS 43–47, TEXTURE

43 Two melodic sentences, made up of four phrases played on flute.

44 Mini concerto for flute and orchestra, with the same sentences being used as from Track 43.

45 'I can stretch . . .' melody line with chord accompaniment only.

46 Extremes of high and low played together in an avant-garde piece.

47 Computer version of the madrigal 'The silver swan'.

TRACKS 48–53, SOUND AND SYMBOL MATCHING

48 Vocal track 'pisst pisst blip pisst' twice.

49 Vocal sounds, first loud and then quieter to match the symbols of figure 47.

50 Vocal sounds to match figure 48.

51 Using classroom instruments to follow the journey in the cartoon of figure 49.

52 Vocal sounds to match the symbols in figure 51.

53 See figure 52. Line (a) spoken with claps, then line (b) and both together.

TRACKS 54–57, GRIDS

54 Each line of the grid is played as shown in figure 54. The grid is played twice, each instrument played independently, then the grid is played twice more with all the instruments played together but without the triangle.

55 The grid in figure 55 is played through as written (four times).

56 a) With count in, and accompaniment.
    b) With count in, the grid is played with the prepared accompaniment.

57 Vocal pattern from grid figure 56 (repeated three times).

TRACKS 58–65, SOUNDS MATCHING WORDS AND PICTURES

58 Vocal sounds for the words in figure 57.

59 Composition using the sounds, see figure 58.

60 Three sounds set in representing the pictures in figure 59.

61 Two sound pictures taken from the pictures in figure 60.

62 Reading the score at figure 61.

63 Telephones alive, see figure 62.

64 The trio picture from the score of figure 63.

65 'In the darkness' chime bar accompaniment to the vocal line in figure 64.

TRACKS 66–71 (CHAPTER 3)

66 Jasvinda's pattern based around a triangle.

67 Children's recorder music arranged in 'Tudor' style.

68 Excerpt of a jazz sequence (as previously heard in track 2).

69 a) Cornet player's improvisation using ideas from the previous jazz piece.

    b) Child playing marimba, repeating a rhythmic sequence from the jazz piece.

70 AKLOWA drumming sequence.

71 Pupils' version on classroom instruments and cardboard boxes.

TRACKS 72–73 (CHAPTER 6)

72 Four pupils perform their first attempt at a particular composition.

73 The same four pupils return to rehearse their composition for a performance in assembly. (See the transcript of their dialogue as they prepare for this occasion, p. 94.)

Appendix: Planning and evaluation checklists

One possible way of recording observations on checklists

☐ Not present on day of evaluation (blank box)
△ Present, no real participation observed
▲ Present and participated
⊞ Present, participated *with* enthusiasm
✦ Present, participated *with* enthusiasm *and* showed musical insight

PLANNING AND EVALUATION CHECKLIST

PLANNING SCHEDULE

KEY STAGE: 1

CLASS YEAR: 1

MUSICAL ELEMENTS	SINGING	PLAYING	MOVING	CREATING	DIRECTING	LISTENING	TEACHER'S COMMENTS
Beat – implied or evident pulse/beat							
no obvious pulse/beat							
maintaining a steady beat							
vocabulary							
Rhythm – rhythmic pattern of words							
patterns for types of movement							
walking							
running							
skipping							
visual representations							
vocabulary							
Structure – (patterns) same/different							
repitition							
beginning/ending							
vocabulary							
Expressive Qualities							
Dynamics – loud/quiet							
contrasts							
Tempo – fast/slow							
contrasts							
vocabulary							
Timbre (tone colour) –							
how sounds are made (shake, blow etc.)							
recognition by sound							
families of instruments (wood, metal etc.)							
vocabulary							
Pitch – high/low							
contrasts							
melodic shapes							
vocabulary							

PLANNING AND EVALUATION CHECKLIST

PLANNING SCHEDULE

KEY STAGE: 1

CLASS YEAR: 2

MUSICAL ELEMENTS	SINGING	PLAYING	MOVING	CREATING	DIRECTING	LISTENING	TEACHER'S COMMENTS
Beat – recognition of							
accent							
Rhythm – rhythmic patterns							
rests							
vocabulary							
visual representation							
Structure – phrases same/different							
beginnings/endings							
questions/answers							
echo							
vocabulary							
Expressive Qualities							
Dynamics – loud/quiet gradations							
place of silence for effect							
Tempo – fast/slow gradations							
flowing/smooth (legato) sounds							
short/pointed (staccato) sounds							
visual representation/graphic notation							
vocabulary							
Timbre (tone colour) –							
identification of sound source							
description of sounds							
vocabulary							
Pitch – melodic shapes ascending/ descending							
melodic movement, steps, strides, jumps							
higher/lower phrases							
forms of vocabulary notation/ representation							
Texture – one sound/several							

PLANNING AND EVALUATION CHECKLIST

PLANNING SCHEDULE

KEY STAGE: 2

CLASS YEAR: 3

MUSICAL ELEMENTS	SINGING	PLAYING	MOVING	CREATING	DIRECTING	LISTENING	TEACHER'S COMMENTS
Duration (beat & rhythm) –							
beat/accent							
same/longer/shorter values							
silence/rests							
repeated rhythmic pattern							
combination of beat and rhythm							
vocabulary							
graphic representation notation							
Structure – phrases same/different							
introductions/endings							
repeated/contrasted sections							
repeat signs:							
Expressive Qualities							
Dynamics – gradual changes							
Tempo – gradual changes							
vocabulary							
symbols – notation							
Style – music for different occasions, various cultures							
Timbre – identification of instruments, applied use for effect							
vocabulary							
Pitch – direction of melody							
melodic shape							
steps, strides, jumps							
repeated sounds							
graphic/conventional notation							
Texture/Harmony –							
presence/absence accompanying sounds							
vocabulary							

EVALUATION CHECKLIST

<u>PLANNING SCHEDULE</u>

KEY STAGE: 2

CLASS YEAR: 4

MUSICAL ELEMENTS	SINGING	PLAYING	MOVING	CREATING	DIRECTING	LISTENING	TEACHER'S COMMENTS
Duration (beat and rhythm) –							
relationship of note values and rests							
metre							
beat and rhythm in combination							
Time signatiures							
vocabulary							
graphic/conventional notation							
Structure – sections repeated/contrasted							
repeat signs							
phrases same/different							
two-part form							
vocabulary							
Expressive Qualities							
Dynamics – changes in dynamics							
Tempo – changes in tempo							
symbols/marks							
Style – music from other cultures							
music from other times							
Texture – thick and thin							
vocabulary							
Timbre (tone colour) –							
use of different instruments for effort							
vocabulary							
Pitch – direction of melody							
treble clef							
melodic phrases same/different							
tonal centre							
vocabulary							
Harmony – use of chords							
tonal centres							
vocabulary							

PLANNING AND EVALUATION CHECKLIST

PLANNING SCHEDULE

KEY STAGE: 2

CLASS YEAR: 5

MUSICAL ELEMENTS	SINGING	PLAYING	MOVING	CREATINGING	DIRECTING	LISTENING	TEACHER'S COMMENTS
Duration (beat and rhythm) –							
rhythmic phrases same/different							
changes in metre							
2:1 note value relationships							
syncopation							
vocabulary							
notation							
Structure – phrases similar/different							
sections contrasting/similar							
two part form							
vocabulary							
Expression Qualities							
Dynamics – changes/effects							
Tempo – changes/effects							
expressive words/symbols							
Style – instrumental combinations and music from other cultures music from other times							
Texture – texture thick/thin							
vocabulary							
graphic/conventional notation							
Timbre (tone colour)							
recognition of different instrument							
association with cultural and historic							
events and times							
Pitch – tonal centre							
melodic phrases							
role of keys/symbols							
vocabulary							
graphic/conventional notation							
Harmony – harmonic texture							
unaccompanied melodies							
melodies with chords							
two or more melodies together							

EVALUATION CHECKLIST

PLANNING SCHEDULE

KEY STAGE: 2

CLASS YEAR: 6

MUSICAL ELEMENTS	SINGING	PLAYING	MOVING	CREATING	DIRECTING	LISTENING	TEACHER'S COMMENTS
Duration (beat and rhythm) –							
rhythmic patterns and phrases							
$^6_8$ compound metre							
3:1 note relationship							
syncopation							
accent and rhythm patterns							
graphic/conventional notation							
relationship between beat							
Structure – phrases similar/different							
contrasting sections							
Rondo form ABAC							
vocabulary							
Expression Quantities							
Dynamics – dynamic symbols							
Tempo – expression marks							
vocabulary							
Style – mood							
style of music culture/period/place							
instrumental groups							
Timbre (tone colour) –							
identification of instruments							
vocabulary							
Pitch – melodic phrases							
sharps/flats/naturals							
pentatonic scale							
vocabulary							
graphic/conventional notation							
Harmony – harmonic texture							
hearing chord changes							
anticipating chord changes							

Bibliography

CHAPTER 1

Bridge, F. (1918) *A Westminster Pilgrim*, Novello and Co., London.

Brocklehurst, B. (1962) *Music in Schools*, Routledge and Kegan Paul, London.

Hill, M.D. and Hill, R. (1834) 'Plans for the Government and Liberal Education of Boys in Large Numbers', printed for C. Knight, Pall Mall East.

HMI (1985) *Curriculum Matters 4 – Music from 5 to 16*, HMSO, London.

Mainwaring, J. (1954) *Teaching Music in Schools*, Paxton and Co., London.

McNair Report (1944) HMSO.

Mellor, David, as Secretary of State for National Heritage for the *National Music Day*, March 1992, as published in *Britain's Culture Begins with Education* by UK Council for Music Education and Training, edited by Larry Westland CBE.

Moulton, Helen (1992) *Multicultural Education Review*, No 14, Winter, Birmingham City Council, Education Department.

NCC (1992) *National Curriculum Council Consultation Report – MUSIC.*

Porteous (1811) *Works*, Vol VI, Cadwell & Davis.

Rousseau's *Emile* translated by W.H. Payne (1906) Book II Sidney Appleton, London.

Swanwick, K. (1992) as Chair of UKCMET (UK Council for Music Education and Training) *Newsletter*, February.

Swanwick, K. and Taylor, D. (1982) *Discovering Music*, Batsford, London.

Taylor, D. (1979) *Music Now*, Oxford University Press, London.

Winn, C. (1954) *Teaching Music*, Oxford University Press, London.

CHAPTER 2

Blacking, J. (1976) *How Musical Is Man?*, Faber and Faber, London.

Clark, V. (1991) *High Low Dolly Pepper*, A. and C. Black, London.

DES (1991) *Music for All Ages*, Final Report of Working Party on Music, August.

Leonhard, C. (1982) 'Humanising Music in a Mechanized Society' in *Music Educators Journal*, May (MENC).

Meyer, L.B. (1971) 'Universalism and relativism in the study of ethnic music', in P. David (ed.) *Readings in Ethnomusicology*, McAllester.

Pellicer, C. (1982) 'Making music in the primary school: report of a course attended at which Marjorie Glynne-Jones was speaking, in *Music in Harrow Schools*, Report No. 8.

Swanwick, K. (1979) *A Basis for Music Education*, NFER Pub. Co.

Swanwick, K. (1988) *Music, Mind and Education*, Routledge, London.

Tait, M. and Haack, P. (1984) *Principles and Processes of Music Education*, Teachers College Press, Columbia University.

CHAPTER 3

Bentley, A. (1966) *Musical Ability in Children and its Measurement*, Harrap, London.

Bruce, T. (1987) *Early Childhood Education*, Hodder & Stoughton, London.

Bruner, J.S. (1966) *Toward a Theory of Instruction*, Harvard University Press, Cambridge, Mass.

Bruner, J.S. (1977) 'Introduction' in B. Tizard and D. Harvey (eds) *The Biology of Play*, London Spastics International Medical Publications.

Bruner, J.S. (1960) *The Process of Education*, MA, Harvard Univerity Press.

Child, D. (1985) 'The growth of intelligence and creativity in young children' in A. Branthwaite and D. Rogers (eds) *Children Growing Up*, Open University Press, Milton Keynes.

Claxton, G. (1984) *Live and Learn. An Introduction to the Psychology of Growth and Change in Everyday Life*, Open University Press, Milton Keynes.

Cobbson, F. (1982) (Audio Cassette) AKLOWA – African Traditional Village.

Davies, C. (1986) 'Say it till a song comes (reflections on songs invented by children 3–13)', *British Journal of Music Education*, **3** (3),
279–93.

DES (1992) *Music: National Curriculum Document*.

Garvey, C. (1977) *Play*, Fontana, London.

Glover, J. and Ward, S. (eds) (1993) *Teaching Music in the Primary School*, Cassell.

Hanks, P. (ed.) (1979) *Collins Dictionary of English Language*.

Lewis, M. (1982) 'Play as whimsy', *Behavioural and Brain Sciences*, **5**, 166.

Moyles, J.R. (1989) *Just Playing*, Oxford University Press, Milton Keynes.

Plummeridge C. (1991) *Music Education in Theory and Practice*, Falmer Press.

Seashore, C. (1938) *Psychology of Music*, McGraw-Hill, New York.

Swanwick, K. and Tillman, J. (1986) 'The sequence of musical development: a study of children's composition', *British Journal of Music Education*, **3** (3), 331.

Wing, H. (1948) 'Tests of musical ability and appreciation', *British Journal of Psychology*, Monograph supplement, vol. 27.

CHAPTER 4

Barnes, D. (1976) *From Communication to Curriculum*, Penguin, London.

Bennett, N., Wragg, T. and Carré, C. (eds) (1991) 'Primary teachers and the National Curriculum', in *Junior Education*, November 1991, Scholastic Publications.

Bloom, B.S. (1956) *Taxonomy of Educational Objectives*, Handbook 1 (Cognitive Domain), Longman, London.

Brown, G. and Wragg, T. (1993) *Questioning* 'Classroom Skills Series', Routledge, London.

Bruner, J. (1960) *The Process of Education*, MA, Harvard University Press.

Dillon, J.J. (1981) To question or not to question in discussions' in *Journal of Teacher Education*, 32, 51–5.

Elliott, J. (1976) *Developing Hypotheses about Classrooms from Teachers' Practical constructs – an account of the work of the Ford Teaching Project*, North Dakota Group on Evaluation, University of North Dakota.

Galton, M., Simon, B. and Croll, P. (1980) *Inside the Primary Classroom*, Routledge and Kegan Paul, London (Reporting on ORACLE project).

Gipps, C. (1992) *What we know about effective primary teaching*, London File, Institute of Education, University of London.

Nelson, D. (1993) 'Co-ordinating music in the Primary School' in J. Glover and S. Ward (eds) *Teaching Music in the Primary School*, Cassell, London.

Struthers, d'R. (ed.) (1991) *A Closer Look at Classrooms*, Middlesex University.

Struthers, d'R. (ed.) (1992) *A Closer Look at Children*, Middlesex University.

Tait, M. and Haack, P. (1984) *Principles and Processes of Music Education*, Teachers College Press, Columbia University, New York.

Wragg, T. and Bennett, N. (1988–91) Directors Leverhulme Primary Project, based at Exeter University: *Classroom Skills Series* of publications based on findings.

CHAPTER 5

Montgomery, D. (1989) *Managing Behavioural Problems*, Hodder & Stoughton, London.

CHAPTER 6

Brocklehurst, B. (1962) *Music in Schools*, Routledge and Kegan Paul, London.

Duncan, A. and Dunn, W. (1989) *What primary teachers should know about Assessment*, Hodder & Stoughton, London.

Gipps, C. (1993) 'Policy making and the use and misuse of evidence' in C. Chitty and B. Simon (eds) *Education Answers Back: Critical Responses to Government Policy*, Lawrence and Wishart, (ed.) London.

Gulbenkian Foundation (1982) *The Arts in schools*, Calouste Gulbenkian Foundation.

Hopkins, D. (1985) *A Teacher's Guide to Classroom Research*, Open University Press.

MANA (1986) *Assessment and Progression in Music Education*, Music Advisers' National Association.

NCC (1992) *Music: Non-Statutory Guidance* (E1).

Plummeridge, C. (1991) *Music Education in Theory and Practice*, Falmer Press.

UKCMET Guidelines for Music in National Curriculum (1993).

Walker, R. and Adelman, C. (1975) *A Guide to Classroom Observation*, Methuen and Co. Ltd, London.

CHAPTER 7

Butler, G. and Barker, M. (1978) *Start Playing Creative Keyboard*, Wise Publications, London.

Cleall, C. (1980) 'Notes towards the clarification of creativity in music education', *Psychology of Music* 8 (2), 44–7.

Glover, J. and Ward, S. (1993) 'Changing music' in J. Glover and S. Ward (eds) *Teaching in the Primary School*, Cassell, London.

Laurence, F. (1990) 'Ideas about singing technique with children' in *African Madonna*, Cambridge University Press, cited in Knight, H. (1992) 'Singing in class music with special reference to children in the Junior school age range' *submitted MA (Mus Ed) thesis*, Institute of Education, University of London.

Mills, J. (1991) *Music in the Primary School*, Cambridge University Press, Cambridge.

Moore, S. and Kemp, A. (1991) 'Effects of nationality and gender on speaking frequency, singing range and preferred tessitura of children from Australia, England and the United States', *Canadian Journal of Research in Music Education*, **33**, Special ISME RE. Edition Dec., 149–56.

Index
